Doorway

to Spiritual Awakening

Becoming Partakers of the Divine

by Theodore J. Nottingham

Book One of

The Transformational Wisdom Series

© 2014 Theosis Books

ISBN 978-0692211694

Printed in the United States of America.

Dedication

To spiritual seekers everywhere, especially those whose journeys have brought us together for a time, to my many Teachers from various Traditions, and with appreciation to the anonymous ones who have supported and sustained me in the desert, with special thanks to A. for the generous efforts that enabled the creation of this work.

Note from the Author:

In the online international spiritual teaching group, *Inner Work for Spiritual Awakening*, we have members at every level on a developmental path of practical psychological and spiritual instruction. The teachings are intended to help you know yourself more objectively, purify your behavior and apply practical, perennial methods and instructions leading to increased consciousness, compassion and wisdom.

This book, the first of the Transformational Wisdom Series, contains some of the rare teaching material that I have shared with my students. Much of it is response to individual questions with additional comments added. By presenting this information in book form, seekers are offered the opportunity to apply these teachings to their specific circumstances in daily life and to find a path toward their deeper Self.

Consider this book, and the others in this series, as tools of learning based on rare knowledge, as well as reference books for your own spiritual journey. The aim is to offer you, the reader, hard to find material which you can review if you have done studies in some of these areas, and to offer you a learning process at a pace that suits your needs.

For addition ongoing guidance, motivation, weekly teachings, and new discoveries consider joining our group at http://innerworkforspiritualawakening.com

Table of Contents

Introduction

Our Ultimate Potential

The human potential is so much more than we can imagine. Our culture tells us that it is about climbing the ladder, financial success, developing our careers, using our various gifts to contribute to the gross national product. Yet for several millennia the true potential for we children of the universe -- made of the dust of stars and connected with all that exists -- has included so much more.

For instance, in the sources of ancient Christian teachings, there is a mysterious word at the heart of their theology known as *"Theosis."* This word, unknown to the West until recently, translates as divinization, deification, or God-realization and makes the point that human beings -- in our short journey through space and time – to discover our union with the Sacred. At the heart of our deepest identity is a divine spark, the core of the universe itself.

Most of us have heard that we are "made in the image of God" but have given it little reflection. We have certainly rarely understood that this image (imago Dei) is meant to be awakened and expanded until it fills us with the consciousness of being a dwelling place for the Uncreated. For rational westerners, this is almost unimaginable and yet it has always been our true purpose. In ancient times, the temple at Delphi proclaimed "Know Thyself" and the Greek philosophers made it their central theme, because it the knowing of one's true Self, we discover not a name or a lineage, but a whole new dimension of what it means to be human. In our very mortality is embedded something of the eternal. Encased within the bones and sinews that are destined to disintegrate is Spirit that comes from beyond and returns home when we are "born into Heaven" as the Orthodox say, or when we cross that threshold.

These ideas cannot be reduced to mere belief systems and dogmas. They have been vividly part of the human experience from the beginning. Those who have known near death events have tasted something from the beyond. I have had the privilege of knowing such intimate experiences with a few friends and I share one with you in particular, which makes it clear that there is so much more to us than our three dimensional senses and our secular world would make us believe:

My friend had died of a heart attack brought on by terrible stress and the persecutions of an institution that rejected him and his worldview mercilessly. They had accomplished their purpose. He could not be fired, but he could be pushed over the edge psychologically and physically. The peer pressure worked beyond their expectations and their toxic work environment literally killed him. This was confirmed by doctors and nurses caring him for him in his last moments.

My friend tells me that he witnessed the scene in the hospital room as though his consciousness had risen out of his body and was watching everyone from the vantage point of the ceiling. He could see the doctors and nurses hurrying about, and he could also see his body – motionless and very pale. Then, all of a sudden, his awareness was gone from the room. He was someplace else – in nature it seems. He vividly remembers flying over trees and woodlands, perhaps the landscape of his native land, unseen for half a century. As he moved swiftly over the countryside, he became aware of a shimmering lake up ahead. As he flew closer, he realized that it was a lake made of light! His whole being was filled with a great eagerness to fly into that lake, to merge with that light. The spiritual zeal of a lifetime was on fire with the desire to "come home."

Just as he was about to plunge into that wondrous light, he felt a strong force pulling upon him. This force was pulling him back, resisting his desire to fly into the beckoning   lake of light. He struggled against this interference with his great yearning. He could already feel the warmth of that mysterious dimension enveloping him. But the force was too strong and he began to sense that he was being taken back, away from that place he so dearly wanted to enter. This "gravitational force" brought him back into the hospital room, and then into his body…and he was alive again.

My friend told me, without that shadow of a doubt, that he knew the nature of that force. This man had a Ph.D. and was a well-respected university professor, author of many scholarly articles. But he knew something that was beyond the limits of his rational mind. He told me that this force which kept him from going into the light forever, and which brought him back into this world to live another two decades, was *the prayers of his friends begging for him to live a while longer!* He knew this with every fiber of his being.

This experience, and so many others like it, is proof positive that our identity and the roots of our being come from a much more profound place than we could imagine or understand. This is why people by the millions yearn for a deeper spiritual encounter with the depths of Reality, one that transcends religions, philosophies, or any other human thought or belief. There is a knowledge buried within that is our compass to a vaster Self whose potential knows no boundaries.

Once we recognize this amazing potential, let us not keep it on a theoretical level. Each day, each moment is an opportunity to break through and experience this truth of our true destiny. Certain masters have called it "becoming transparent to the Divine" and the spiritual practices of many teachings help us to find our way through the fog of the illusions we have about ourselves. For our petty pride, our silly vanity, our fears and anxieties keep us from discovering that ever shining sun at the heart of our being. That is where we find the peace that transcends all circumstances, the peace that "no one understands" in this chaotic world of ours. This inner peace cannot be disturbed by anything, neither illness nor unemployment nor death itself.

Discover, then, that real potential, that real purpose for the meaning of life, for in doing so you will know that you are an integral part of this universe, so much more than the needs and habits of our body and the limitations of our mind. We are that drop in the ocean of the cosmos which contains within itself the entire cosmos. May you taste of that consciousness and find your true identity.

PART ONE

*"You understood him from the point of view of Time, but he spoke
to you from the point of view of Eternity"*

From John Tauler, disciple of

Meister Eckhart, during his Teacher's excommunication trial

1

Rediscovering Christianity

What does it mean to be a Christian in the twenty-first century? There's so much baggage associated with this religion; it has been so misrepresented in the media around us in our time and in the centuries before us. Many people point to the horrors and bloodshed committed in the name of religion and so they throw the baby out with the bathwater as is said.

They disregard the content, the power within these teachings because of what human beings have made of them, turning them into institutions of power full of distortions. It is amazing that the wisdom, the life-transforming power within Christianity, is still available, is still around after two thousand years of abuse – going back to the very beginning when the church in Jerusalem thought that it was only for them, only for their people – the struggles between Peter and Paul. That sensed-based human dimension of our character has hijacked the universal, eternal Teaching made known by the Christ, the Anointed One, whose intimate relationship with the I Am at the heart of the universe made all the difference for those who could grasp what was offered.

In this world of chaos and brokenness, I challenge you to reconsider from a whole new perspective what it might mean to be a "Christian." As you may know, the word "Christian" was applied by outsiders to those who followed the Way of Christ. Among them, originally, they knew each other as "People of the Way." A way – a new way of living, a new way of being, a new way of understanding the world, a new quality of consciousness (to put it in modern language).

Much of the dogma of the Church, as the great scholar of mystical Christianity Evelynn Underhill put it, is a poor attempt to express *experience*. The whole mystery of the Trinity came out from Gregory of Nazianzen seeking to poetically express his own experience of wonder. It is up to each of us to *taste and see* – to rediscover for ourselves what is really offered in these transformational revelations.

We have to put aside the devastating misrepresentations of history, the absurdities that have created layers and layers of misunderstandings and contradictions. At the Source, it was originally all about illumination and light and joy. "*I tell you this that my joy may be made complete,*" says the Christ.

Imagine a Teaching that speaks of the mystery at the heart of creation as "*Abba,*" as "Daddy," with an intimacy and a self-surrender in utter trust which generates transcendent courage, transcendent love – Unconditional Love incarnated in the world.

Christianity was never meant to be an exclusive type of religion. It is, in fact, the apex of human intuition. It is the ultimate expression of that potential within each of us *to be our spiritual selves awakened in the world* – channels of blessing to the world. Perhaps you've known people with that kind of light in their eyes, that kind of astonishing love that heals, renews, because of their own love of that which is holy. In this twenty-first century we have lost touch with not only the roots of these teachings, but with the very sense of the Sacred and the Holy. We have reduced our reality to the most mundane and superficial sense-based, three dimensional box. We have made impotent that which is the very source of our life within us and around us. We've lost sight of the visible within the invisible. So I urge you not to throw it out just because of what you see on television – because of the fragmentation of sects that have created another religion and called it Christianity.

Absurdities such as the Scope's trial, the argument of the seven days of creation versus science, was never an issue. The ancient writings of the Hebrew people contained profound mystical symbolism. For instance, the number seven represents the perfection of God. There never was a contradiction between spirituality and science. Quantum physicists have begun to understand this fact. The Scriptures were never meant to be read on the surface – the literal interpretation was never the teaching across the centuries. Fundamentalism comes out of extraordinary ignorance and disconnection with the whole legacy of Christianity. The great teachers of the Faith spoke of spiritual preparation to approach these teachings so that intuition would be part of our experience. There was an awareness of a difference between the Old and the New Testament. As Jesus says, *"You have heard it said, but I say to you…"* Something new, a new revelation of the Uncreated One was presented. We can't throw it all together with the wrathful, jealous God of primitive times. Something dramatically different has taken place and yet many have thrown it all together as one book and confused everybody. Take the time to look into these matters and to rediscover for yourself so that it isn't stolen from you.

Have the integrity to find out what it really says – what is really taught – what Meister Eckhart of the fourteenth century had to say about it - what John of the Cross and Teresa of Ávila, Isaac the Syrian and the Desert Fathers – or Thomas Merton of the twentieth century. So many haters of this religion only understand it at its most absurd level – only take some literalistic view and assume that is Christianity and then criticize it. They claim intelligence and yet they won't use their own mind to really understand and incorporate what it is that is presented here. In this day and age when it is so necessary to rediscover the depths, meaning and purpose in our lives, let's re-examine what this is all about. Let's go beyond the Roman version of the West and see what the East teaches. This is where we find this idea of *theosis* -- divinization, God realization, which is so much more dynamic in its theology and its wisdom. We in the West have been cut off from that for so long.

We now live in a global community where all becomes available and we can discover that we are not merely children of the American frontier or of the European creeds, but of the very origins. Then you will find that there is a mighty power, a non-exclusive, eternal dimension that actually can change your psychology, your joy of life; it can lift you up, give you a sense of self beyond anything you imagined to empower you to become that child of the universe, a child of God to whom miracles of goodness can come. Take the time to seek; take the time to rediscover the depths of these teachings and everything will change.

20

2

Inner Warfare

We need to engage all that we are in order for transformation to take place. So we have here a student who shares with us those personal details: "I have recently had some minor success in maintaining self-observation through a sustained period." I hope you all know what that means – inner separation, watching objectively, not being the selves, the "I"s that are passing through as thoughts and feelings. The person further defines it by saying, "… by that I mean semi-continuously for a few days," which in itself is significant work because it requires the strength of will power to focus attention enough that it be intentionally used, intentionally divided, so that there is a part that remains within and observes the rest, as opposed to just being scattered and lost as we usually are.

Then we find out more of this person's experience: "However, immediately upon noticing this positive effect," (which is a liberation of anxiety and worry and fear)"… succeeding days have been plagued with turmoil. My brief period of greater awareness seems far behind and now." That is a period of greater awareness, which I hope each of you has tasted because these teachings will take you there quickly if you apply them. "I am in more turmoil than before - seemingly unable to see clearly as though I'm walking in a sand storm. Out of nowhere - negative emotions have entered - seemingly slipping in the back door." Very interesting metaphor. "I guess I am observing this too but certainly not with any confidence or clarity."

So, here's the question: "Does this flood of negative 'I's' and general internal commotion, often follow a period of Work 'success'?" That is a very valuable question for anyone who has any experience with these transformational ideas. Once you have tasted their power and seen what they can do for you, then we're on the same page. And sure enough, teachers from a variety of traditions, for instance Karlfried Graf Durkheim -- who began with Zen Buddhism, Meister Eckhart, Christian Mysticism -- that great teacher assures us that twenty-four hours won't go by after a great experience of transcendent being without something dark and negative occurring. Something fights back! We don't need to get metaphysical about it - or mythical - imagining what that could be. That is not necessary, because we are focused right now on the phenomena that we are observing.

One reason for this occurrence which you will discover is that, after serious effort, there is this flood of wrong work because internal warfare is going on. The false personality, the petty ego, the illusions of self that have run the show do not want to let go of their power. We are not unified. That is a foundational concept in this great teaching and you find it reflected in the teachings of Christ everywhere. We are legion, in fact. Out of all this fragmentation, there is that little baby bird within that wants, yearns and hungers for the purity of awakening consciousness which is not concerned with just oneself and one's survival in the material world. It is, therefore, unnecessary for basic animal existence.

Then there is that much larger part within each of us which has only that interest. Not to speak of our being brainwashed unconsciously by culture, parents, and one's own misguided filters on Reality. Once you have truly begun these efforts, and started the struggle, you discover that you have an adversary. But the adversary doesn't have horns and a tail and a pitchfork. The adversary is you, the enemy is within.

The enemy is all that which wants to maintain its authority within you and knows that it is threatened. The very success you have had in cleansing, in purifying, in pacifying, in helping essence arise, is an assault on false personality, which has been king of the hill all along. This spiritual warfare is very specifically mapped out in early Easter Orthodox Christianity. The books of their great Illumined Ones (they call them "God-Bearers or Grace-filled") are full of such teaching: *Inner Warfare, The Path to Salvation, The Philokalia, The Arena* -- these masterpieces of authentic Christian spiritual teachings,

24

much of them for monks who had totally committed themselves to this transformation, are meant for all people.

They are reflected in this Fourth Way which does not take place in a monastery. We use life itself as the school in which this occurs, the battlefield if you will. So don't be surprised that it is a war and you will have to decide who is going to win. You will have to strengthen that part of you that wants to be God-centered, that wants to reach those higher spheres of God-consciousness and behavior that can care for others without need for rewards or pats on the back. We have no idea yet, without real awakening, how we are slaves to these automatic features of ours that come with the package.

It is against the current battle, like the salmon jumping upstream – nothing less. It is against the natural way. But that has always been the case; that is how it must be. We are struggling to awaken, unify and strengthen the spiritual Self within us – the divine spark that has been buried away, so that it can have control over the body, so that we can use our powers for good. Many have accomplished this, but always at a high price – whether it is personal suffering or suffering that has just come by circumstance. Rather than being broken by it, such people have used it as empowerment, as motivation for rising above, for not being dragged down. But be sure that you will always be fighting the lower within you which seeks to drag you down. You must be vigilant.

Vigilance, watchfulness, "Watch! Do not sleep," is virtually unique to the Christ's teachings. No one emphasized that so strongly and that is why we have to use every tool we can, including listening to those who have gone ahead, creating 'alarm clocks' for ourselves (as Gurdjieff calls them) which remind us and re-align us with what we are trying to do. This requires an all or nothing commitment. As the ribald, exotic Gurdjieff would say, you have to 'go whole hog including the postage.' Otherwise your vanity will always win out, your instinctive center will run the show and you will end up buried and disappearing like everybody else. We are creating something that lives on. It is that simple, that awesome, that demanding.

This is why Christianity is a religion of sacrifice, centered on the crucifixion – not as some general atonement for everybody -- which is a complete misunderstanding -- but as the expression of the fact that we must crucify the lower for the higher.   Then a new life begins for us. It is can be done with the help of Spirit, but know that it is always a struggle. Perhaps the time will come when it won't be so intense, but we must always be on our guard because the wolf is always at the door within. Such has been the spiritual history of humanity from the beginning.

3

Conquering Yourself

One of the great verses in Holy Scripture is, "All things work together for good for those who love God." I hope that some of you have found comfort over the years with that incredible saying, even though it is very hard to understand. What does it mean? Does God allow bad things to happen so that good can come out of it? No, that's not what it means.

There was a book written a little while ago that is still popular, *When Bad Things Happen to Good People*. The implied question is: Why do bad things happen to good people? That assumes that God is making bad things happen to us. It comes out of a common presupposition that God is a big clock maker who controls everything

29

and we just have to go through it. The real question is: *How does good come out of bad, which happens to people?* Over the years when I have counseled folks going through hard times, I have found that those who have no connection with God, no sense of God, have no way out. The human mind cannot work through the paradox of hard times and unfair times to find good. It takes something else; and we can find that something else in these scriptures. "All things work together for good for those who love God," and that is further qualified by the words, "who are called according to His purpose." And that is further qualified, "for those whom He predestined…"

When John Calvin in 1500 studied those words, he made a mess of them. He concluded that there are those who are predestined and there are those who are not. Now does that sound like the teachings of Jesus to you? He who came for everyone? He who was a universal representation of God's goodness to the world. He didn't choose a few and leave the others to die a miserable death. He came for all of us. And what does that mean? Each and every one of you *is called*. You are each called to find God; you are each designed to be able to do so. Not only that, but each one of you was foreknown. Before you were born, your Maker knew you. Before you had a name, before you had a social security number, before you wore glasses, before you went to school, you were known and loved and you were *called according to His purpose.* And what is that purpose? "To be conformed to the likeness of His Son!"

You are meant to exist on this planet so that you can be conformed to the likeness of His Son. We have made a big mistake removing Jesus so far from us that we can't reach Him. He seems so different. The fact is that we are told that He is *our template*; we are meant to become like Him. He is not an impossible miracle worker; He is the firstborn of a large family – of a family seeking to become like Him. That is the definition of a Christian. But something gets in the way. So the question becomes: What is it in us that does not want to conform to His likeness? And that is why the scriptures say: Seek! Seek Him always. Jesus said, "Seek and you will find."

What is it that keeps us from seeking? This is where we have to get honest and real, because in every one of us, even those of us who love for God – in every one of us there is something that does not want to be called according to His purposes, to be conformed to the likeness of His Son. Do you know what it is? It's that little chunk of self-love that never grew up – that always has to have its own way – that gets offended so easily – that can't stand this, can't stand that – full of likes and dislikes. It's you and me all day long, every day. And we come here to this holy place to hear the sacred scriptures so that we can begin to conquer that part of us and get back into our destiny.

Every one of us, regardless of your education, regardless of our past, is meant to be a new person in Christ. This is not just a nice saying; it's not just a belief -- it's a phenomenon, but we have to get ahold of who we are. We have to face ourselves and not allow that which is uninterested in conforming to this sacred template to rule the nest. This is difficult spiritual effort, but if you put it in context – if you want to be one of those who finds good in suffering, not because God wants us to, but because that's how it is in this little passage through life. We cannot avoid it, but we can find meaning, we can find strength through suffering. There is no question about it. Jesus is the first born of a large family. There have been people in that family down through history – you know some of them, maybe you know some of them that are alive today who have proven to each one of us that we can do it, that we can respond to the call. The little stirring in us that wants something more – that isn't satisfied with the dreariness of ordinary life – is the call of God on your life. So what is it to conquer one's self? Consider the poem *If* by Rudyard Kipling? Let me just give you a few words of it.

"If you can dream - and not make dreams your master;
If you can think - and not make thoughts your aim;
If you can meet with triumph and disaster
And treat those two imposters just the same;
If you can bear to hear the word [truth] you've spoken
Twisted by knaves to make a trap for fools,
Or watch the things you gave your life to broken,
And stoop and build 'em up again with worn out tools;

If you can fill the unforgiving minute
With sixty seconds' worth of distance run -
Yours is the Earth and everything that's in it,"

That's a portrait of conquering one's self. Can you imagine encountering triumph and disaster and dealing with them equally? That means not being a puppet on a string lost in what you like and what you don't like. That means following the first commandment. You all know the first commandment don't you? Hear oh Israel! The Lord your God is one, and you will love the lord your God with all your what? All your heart, all your mind, all your strength, all your soul. We don't do that. We're busy being self-absorbed, self-interested, and unhappy.

Do you know that we are full of addictions? And I don't mean the usual ones. There are people who are addicted to being unhappy; they don't know who they are unless they're unhappy. There are people who are addicted to power; they've got to have control over everybody else. There are people who are addicted to fear; everything frightens them. Each one of us carries some weakness like that. That is the axis around which our personality functions. And it gets us nowhere and it makes us miserable and it ruins our relationships. And I'm here to tell you there's a way out – there's supposed to be a way out. We are predestined and called to a way out. That isn't the way God wants us to live and we have the tools to change it.

We are meant to become internally free. But that requires us to be vulnerable doesn't it? You know why most of us love that big, strong independence thing? Nobody can touch me; nobody needs to help me; nobody can hurt me. You leave everybody out including God. That's a sorry place to be and when suffering comes, you won't find good in it.

The saying is, "All things work together for good," that is to say in spite of what awful things are happening to you, somehow, some way -- if you stay connected to God, if you don't give up on God -- you will find your way through it into something good. Most of us who have been around for a while know the hard truth – that it takes a little suffering to break out of our shell of infantile selfishness – of focus only on ourselves as the center of the universe, and discover ta vaster world and a greater purpose. That old saying which tell us that it is better to give than receive is life-giving. When we shut the valves of life off, we are back to the miserable mediocrity that we know so well. When the hard time come and the bad news about illness comes, we've got no resources because we're all alone in an empty place.

The good news is about being not all alone – but you've got to be willing to let God in so that in fact, everything can work together for good because your life belongs to Him – to be conformed to the likeness of the son.

You know what Jesus did, don't you? You know the story. You know how he said, "Thy will be done." Do you know what strength it takes to do that? To not fall with disaster and rise with triumph? To say at all times, "Thy will be done." My life is given to you. That's not some mystical thing; that's not for clergy; that's for each and every one of us, each in our own way to give back to God what belongs to Him and then life is filled with wonder. Life is no longer just about what we want, what we don't like. It's a wonderful thing because then we encounter God here and now. We no longer live in our fantasies. Do you know how much time we spend daydreaming? Become aware of it next time – next time you're shaving or driving or next time whatever. Maybe right now you're daydreaming. Welcome back! Life is in the present moment. Eternity is the present moment. God is in the present moment. The trick is we're not. We're out of touch with reality. We're always scheming about this, worried about that, angry about this and never here. Never here, never quite enough to be here.

If you get here, you'll find that this gospel wisdom is true. You'll find peace and strength and healing and courage and faith and then you'll make it through suffering. Then you'll know you won't lose sight of the light. You know the saying, "Weeping may last for a night," but what comes in the morning? "Joy!" Joy comes in the morning to those who keep God in their lives. Friends, we've all seen unhappy people. When I was in Oklahoma, I was taken up to the top of a hill and shown barns all around. They told me in every one of those barns someone hung himself out of despair. There is another way. There is another way; we don't have to go down that dark road to nowhere. If we enter on this path that we are called to be on to be conformed to the likeness, than who can be against us? Then good things can be found in spite of what the appearances are. Then you'll understand that all things work for good and all bad things end up good

If God is your path, if God is your life and then you can understand the saying "God is for us. Who can be against us?"

4

Know the Times

[11] And do this, understanding the present time: The hour has already come for you to wake up from your slumber, because our salvation is nearer now than when we first believed. [12] The night is nearly over; the day is almost here. So let us put aside the deeds of darkness and put on the armor of light. [13] Let us behave decently, as in the daytime, not in carousing and drunkenness, not in sexual immorality and debauchery, not in dissension and jealousy.
[14] Rather, clothe yourselves with the Lord Jesus Christ, and do not think about how to gratify the desires of the flesh.

[Romans 13:11-14, NIV]

I'd like to begin with the symbols that are around us. How silly it would be to have symbols we don't understand, just like teachings we don't understand. And for centuries you know that's been the case, otherwise Christians would have been saintly beings from the beginning. So my job is to bring clarity to you, each in your own way — something that you can incorporate into your own life and bring change and renewal. We are not here to stay the same, to live the life that others would impose upon us.

So let me begin with the simple example of light. The reason we have this light [advent candles] here today is because it is the symbol of divine revelation. "I am the light of the world," "the light has come into the world" — so many statements of that nature. It is a metaphysical expression of a truth that is hard to put in words. The divine in the midst of darkness.

Now we can't do darkness right now, but imagine a bit. What is darkness? Two things: darkness is the absence of God. So all of you who know people who live in some strange, barren void, know that this is darkness. So this metaphor becomes a reality that you can witness in their eyes, in their lives. God is absent; the light is not on. Darkness is not only the absence of God, but also the ignorance of God. And boy, do we have plenty of that. We have ignorance of God in churches, not merely among folks trying to learn, but among clergy teaching bad teachings. We are so fragmented now, two thousand plus years later that anything goes. And thank God that in this little remnant of people seeking truth, seeking meaning, you can hear something that resonates for you. Don't take my word for it; let your heart respond. For it will know; your inner teacher will know what is true. Harshness and intolerance and judgment and negativity – that is not the light; that is the darkness. And we live in a very dark time.

You heard me tell about what the tree represents, Spirit rising up in glory to God. Or the wonderful evergreen. Evergreen – sign from ancient times of immortality. Those of you who were so kind to decorate for us – thank you so much. What a delight it was to see so many folks helping out. You didn't know you were putting immortality on the window, did you? But it is a representation that can strengthen our resolve and our faith – God's steadfast eternal love. That's what all this is representing. So, it isn't another Christmas with the same decorations. It is dynamic, cosmic symbolism to help us focus in on what this is all about. As the weeks go by, we'll talk about this here [indicating nativity scene] and what its symbolism is. Perhaps you remember a famous saying from a German mystic, "It doesn't matter if Jesus is born a thousand times in Bethlehem, if he's not born in your heart. So if there's no room at the inn, it isn't the inn in Nazareth, it's the inn right here [indicating heart]. That is the deep teaching.

Let me begin with that marvelous Psalm 130. *"Out of the depths I cry to you, O Lord."* Now tell me something, does that ring a bell for any of you? Haven't we all been there? More than once in our lives. Out of the depths, out of the need, out of our anguish and fear, out of our anger and distress, out of our depths we cry to you oh Lord. Hear my voice – magnificent words of our condition as contemporary today as it was when the psalm was written because human beings are human beings. And that's the glory of it – you can take your personal experience that you know well – maybe nobody else knows it – but you know when you've been in that dark place and now you know that other have been there and have answers for us. We are not alone; we are not left orphan.

The teaching in the Old Testament goes on to say, "If you oh Lord should mark inequities, who could stand?" What does that mean? Never let it just stay on the page. It's so personal. It means none of us need be held back by guilt, by mistakes and ignorance and wrong-doing – that there is forgiveness – and if each one of us hear knew how much we were forgiven, we would be set free. We would be healed.

There are people who carry guilt and pain for a lifetime. Salvation is healing [*sozo*], fullness of life, and life in abundance. And we learn in this ancient teaching at the dawn of time that this is the kind of Uncreated One and mystery at the heart of the universe who made us. And then we hear a teaching, "Now wait for the Lord. My soul waits." Now it's not like waiting at a bus stop. It's an intentional attentive waiting. It's patience. It's certainty that God will come to help you. Who dares to wait patiently in the midst of distress? That is the way that we are given. That is the spiritual instruction. Wait for the Lord knowingly, expecting that you will have help. If you don't wait, if you run off and give up and say, "Okay, time's up. I tried that; I'm going to do something else - that's what we call outer darkness, you're on your own. Wait for the Lord.

Then we're given this glorious metaphor, "My soul waits more than those who watch for the morning," and how foolish it would be not to understand that simple metaphor. In ancient times there were guards in the towers and you can still see those towers across the landscape of Israel – and those men would stand there all night watching deep into the dark, deep into the cold. We heard about a sore toe today. Imagine their toes after eight hours during the night. They can't wait for the sun to rise. So they use this example of physical strain and effort to say that my soul waits even more than they do for the rising sun, for the appearance of God in our lives.

We don't worship a God over there or up there. We recognize that God, through Christ, is right here, right now and knows our need. And we're told, "Oh Israel – understand this is not a nation, not a political situation, not an ethnic thing. The church took on the word Israel. And the word Church (*Ecclesia*) means: The assembly of those who are called out. In other words, each individual who is called out of a godless world gathers with companions on the Way and becomes part of the Body of Christ together – incarnations of Divine Goodness.

That's Israel spiritually – the remnant. For with the Lord there is steadfast love. Steadfast like these wreathes representing immortality, God's love never aging, never rusting, never turning brown, always green. And with Him is great power to redeem.

Friends, I don't know if that can reach into your depths, but in my line of work I deal with folks almost every day, almost seven days a week - yes, even on my day off, who need a lot of redeeming, who have made a lot of mistakes and to hear these words, "great power to redeem," is water in the desert. And it is true for all of us whether we have done awful things in the past or not. With connection with God is transformation and forgiveness, letting go of the past – starting anew. And each one of us must know that even if our past was oh – just dull and selfish we need that new life, that redemption, that joy. What's the point of listening to that wonderful rendition and not feeling it in your heart? This is not a performance; this is a holy expression of the truth. We can be happy people when nothing is going our way. That is the genius of Christianity – of cosmic truth.

Did you know that something happened between the old and New Testament? They're not quite the same. What happened? Advent. The arrival. Jesus, the Christ. You know in people's live oftentimes we say that there is a before and an after. Something that changes everything.

That's Yeshua. Because with Him comes a whole new level of truth. And through our friend Paul, we get a much more dynamic teaching than even the one you just heard from Psalms. So we take the first line, "So besides this you know what time it is, for it is now the moment for you to wake from sleep." And being a translator, I know that there are so many ways to take an old language and represent it differently, so listen to this one which I got from the Amplified Bible, "Besides this, you know what a critical hour this is. How it is high time now to wake up out of your sleep," which means to rouse to reality. To wake from sleep is to rouse to reality. That's quite a quantum leap isn't it? And here's another translation, "Know the time even now. This very moment is the very time to wake from sleep." I even looked into the French, "It is time to wake up finally from sleep. You must come out of your sleep."

I've described sleep to you before as a spiritual technical term: *Watch, do not sleep. High time to wake from sleep.* It is not sleep on the pillow. Sleep is that state of consciousness of awareness that we are in right now. Now it's true that some of you may be literally asleep, but then there's that other kind of sleep which is barely above what's happening in your bed – where you live in imagination, where reality is filtered through all kinds of silly things, where you're nothing but a stimulus response machine. Push a button, that's what happens.

Don't we know ourselves well enough by now, especially you with white hair? Have you seen how many times the same thing happens again and again and again? If this happens, you do that – sort of like Pavlov's dog. That sleep will hypnotize by external events and there is nothing within that is consistent and constant and focused of God. That inner sanctuary, that place where we can say, here I stand. You will not steal my peace. We can be that strong. The rest of the world is in total chaos. And when you're in that kind of sleep where you have no compass, no direction, that's when all kinds of accidents happen because anything can happen.

Any thought in your mind, any feeling can redirect your life and Jesus is here to save us from that. That's part of salvation because to live centered in the one thing that matters, the one desire of the human heart – out of the depths I cry to you oh Lord is where we must learn to go. Remember, we are here to grow spiritually, first and foremost and to disregard that is to make a mockery of the body of Christ – of these blood-soaked words of the Bible written in prison of the salvific death of Christ. And he goes on, "the night is far gone; the day is near." I've told you about night, about darkness. The day is near. The day is near for each of us who never thought it would be that you could actually be happy in this life. That's the day. The day is God present in your life – not as a belief, not as a dogma – as a reality. As I tell you so often, as an experience. And sometimes we have to hit rock bottom; we have to hit hard times to really taste it. Because if we're doing fine, who needs God? Right?

The trouble is you're only going to do fine for a little while. There will come a day, so you might as well start right now don't you think? Because you don't want to wait until the last minute to try to catch up. Let us the lay aside the works of darkness. Now most of us would be uncomfortable with that if we really thought about it. Works of darkness? Nobody here is evil. If you are, bless you to not be evil. Works of darkness – to put on the armor of light because it's going to take some power to have the courage to struggle against darkness.

Darkness is always trying to overcome the light and what we know from Advent and from the resurrection is that darkness cannot overcome the light. And that is a truth that can carry you into bliss and hope all the days of your life. So he lists this business of laying aside works of darkness: licentiousness, drunkenness, debauchery. Now, maybe with the choir it's different. I don't know — kidding — look at all those innocent people. Most of us here don't have those problems, but then if you get to the end of the sentence, you have quarreling and jealousy. Now that's a little closer to home isn't it? Who doesn't quarrel? Who doesn't pitch a fit? Who doesn't gossip? Who doesn't do all these things that are being watched by God? If we knew we were being seen, maybe we would stop.

It is the ungodly who act any old way and bear the consequences. So, if you have the fear of the Lord, the reverence of the Holy that we celebrate here today, maybe you can keep it under control. Maybe you can say I don't want to go down that road – because God knows. There is nothing that will remain hidden – the light will expose everything so even our very human ways, if they are not pleasing to God, are going to cost us.

The whole point is to find a way to live honorably with purity, with happiness, with righteousness pleasing God. That's the answer; here are the instructions in these sacred writings. Are we going to apply them or not? You know it's like – teachers, we've got a whole bunch of teachers here – you know your kids have to do their homework and I'll admit I took six years of Latin in France and in America, and I can't remember a single thing. So that happens. But here, we've got to remember. It's life and death. Just like the Holy one says, I give you life and death; choose life because it is death to live in quarreling and negativity and gossip and back stabbing and all that stuff that we secretly enjoy.

It's time to face it, especially now at Advent. Let us come into this holy place cleansed, purified. That's how we honor God. That's how we prove our belief in the arrival of the divine in the midst of our lives. God will help the one who seeks to make those efforts. Finally he says, "Put on (or clothe) yourself with the Lord Jesus Christ. Don't think of that as some other unapproachable metaphor. It means think like Him. Live like Him. Not as a vagrant, but as a compassionate person, a forgiving person. Even if you're the only one in the crowd. Don't let the poison of negativity get contagious on you. Recognize it for what it is. Put on Christ, nothing less. Each one of us is called to that. Because in putting on that understanding of life, you find your true self, your true destiny, your true joy. "And make no provision for the flesh." Now that's a little spooky for some I'm sure. You mean I can't have a good glass of wine or things like that? Flesh in Greek is s-a-r-x. It does not mean skin; it means our animal nature, our lower nature, our non-spiritual nature.

Make no provision for that. And those of you who have loved another for many years – and we've got a few of you here – those of you who have learned to care for another at your expense, you know what it means to make no provision for the flesh. You sacrifice, you transcend your needs, your desires, your comfort, for another. God bless you because you are living these instructions. Love is the key. We are designed to live in such a way.

5

Reconciliation

"For this reason, since the day we heard it, we have not ceased praying for you and asking that you may be filled with the knowledge of God's will in all spiritual wisdom and understanding so that you may lead lives worthy of the Lord, fully pleasing to Him as you bear fruit in every good work and as you grown in the knowledge of God.

May you be made strong with all the strength that comes from His glorious power and may you be prepared to endure everything that patience, while joyfully giving thanks to the Father who has enabled you to share in the inheritance of the saints in the light.

He has rescued us from the power of darkness and transferred us into the kingdom of His beloved son in whom we have redemption and forgiveness of sins. He is the image of the invisible God, the first born of all creation for in Him all things of heaven and earth were created — things visible and invisible whether thrones or dominions or rulers or powers. All things have been created through Him and for Him. He, Himself, is before all things and in Him all things hold together. He is the head of the body, the church. He is the beginning, the first born from the dead so that He might come to have first place in everything. For in Him all the fullness of God was pleased to dwell and through Him God was pleased to reconcile to Himself to all things, whether in earth or in heaven by making peace through the blood of His cross."

[A reading from Colossians 1:9-10]

There are many beautiful words here. The danger of beautiful words is that we can just gloss over them, think we've received something because it's like a lovely song and miss what it's really about. Two thirds of the New Testament is filled with letters from Paul. These letters are spiritual instruction to his spiritual children. Paul was the first mystic, the first one to play that role of expanding Christ's mission out to the world without whom we would not be here. Because the first disciples thought it was a Jewish sect; they didn't get it. Paul was inspired by the resurrected Christ to go into all the world and to teach and to help us become that which Christ called us to be. So, my hope today is to take these pretty words and turn them into specific instructions for your life right now. You've heard me say it a million times but there's something extra here today with Thanksgiving. The cornucopia which goes back to Zeus and some Greek mythology, but it represents harvest. We know it represents our forbearers if you will, the Puritans, the beginning.

I just want to make the point as I seek to do on most Thanksgivings - that this moment of thanksgiving which has come down to us was after the harshest winter they had had in that part of the world in ages; it was still the little ice age I am told. I've shared with some of you – if you've got a photographic memory was that I had relatives there; maybe you did to. And my relative through my great, great, great, great, great grandmother in New England was Myles Standish, the Captain of the Mayflower. Why do I say that? Because his beloved wife Rose who came with him along with seventeen other wives to the new world, the new beginning, the freedom of living a new life, had died before Thanksgiving as did those seventeen other women. So these people had suffered greatly, were still in mourning, and yet they gave thanks. It would be silly to leave that out of this picture, wouldn't it? No matter how great the harvest was, no matter how much they managed to get alone with the Native Americans, there was grief of heart and yet they gave thanks. Let that stick in your mind because that is at the heart of this particular teaching which is jammed with information.

So Saint Paul tells us for all time – not the folks in a particular church at a particular time – tells us now out of his revelations that he has not ceased praying for us. And don't you doubt you twenty-first century rationalists that there are prayers made for us in another dimension. And he continues to pray that you may be filled with the love of God's will in all spiritual understanding.

The prayer for each person – whatever you want to label yourself – a disciple – a Christian – a seeker – is to be filled with the knowledge of God's will. Now some of you are going to be filled on Thursday, right? That's part of the deal. So you know what "physically filled" means. Everybody's going to have a stomachache. Am I right? He wants that kind of complete imbuing of the knowledge of God's will for each one of us. And "the knowledge of God's will" in Greek is *epinosis*, which doesn't mean information or intellectual adherence or saying yes to a creed or dogma. *Epinosis* means practical experience of God. He is praying that you will discover practical, tangible experience of the reality of God – so much so that it fills your life. This is a prayer for transformation because most of us don't spend much time trying to be filled with that kind of knowledge. We're too busy making it on our own.

It's very hard to depend on the Holy One. I'm sure everybody here – even you happy singers – have had hard times; that's part of being human. And in those hardest of times to trust in the goodness of God anyway is very difficult; it's going against the rational mind. It's going against perhaps, what your peers are saying and yet, this is what we are called to be.

To know that the will of God, the goodness of God, can be lived out and save us from our miseries with all spiritual wisdom and understanding – the Amplified Bible says, "in comprehensive insight into the ways and purposes of God." Comprehensive insight into the purposes and ways of God, the Uncreated One. That's a tough one; that's getting cosmic. You've got to go big picture and surely you know that sometimes the best way to help your pain (do we all know that – the answer to that?) is to help somebody else. That's one. Another way is to have some relativity, some larger picture of reality. At least we're not in the Philippines right now with no home, with no shelter. But don't you see that if each of us is just locked on to our particular problem, we can't get out of it. And he goes on to say again specific teachings – I'm going to give you four steps because we humans love those seven steps to success, ten steps to losing weight in a month, right? Those books sell like crazy. So he gives us four instructions in this letter.

To lead lives worthy of God, pleasing to God. Now understand this. What does it mean to live lives worthy? Well, first of all it means that we can live lives unworthy and unpleasing to God. Good luck with that. And you know that there's a whole lot of people out there for whom that is the way of life and all of us are always on that edge where we have to make that choice, because an unworthy life, a life that does not seek to please the higher, the good and the beautiful, the pure, the right is going to go the other direction into outer darkness and meaninglessness. We are given saving instructions to keep us from that.

He goes on to say so that you may bear fruit in every good work. And as westerners we assume that means that we do stuff. And it's good to do things. I'm a doer kind of guy. Some of us really like to be "can do" people. But this is not about doing; this is about being. Because what is the fruit He's talking about? The fruit of Holy Spirit. Remember what that is? *Love, joy, peace, patience, goodness, kindness, gentleness, humility, faithfulness, self-control.* That's bearing fruit in the Spirit. Can you imagine if we lived that way? What wonderful people we would be.

Every time we get together we would soak it in. I don't think we're far from that friends. You know I often give sermons that are hard-hitting, but this place is a beautiful place with beautiful people. We are very lucky because there's a whole mess of churches out there that are filled with toxic energy and nastiness and all that is ungodly, and will certainly lead to their demise. We attract Holy Spirit into this place by living these instructions - remembering what the knowledge of God is – filling ourselves with it. Not leaving it in the sanctuary when we walk out the door.

And then he says, "May you be made strong with all the strength that comes from His glorious power." Another sentence that is so pretty that you could just walk right past it. *Made strong with His strength*. In other words we are not expected to do this by ourselves. When you are down for the count, you are not expected to get back up by yourself.

You may have plenty of willpower, but sometimes life just breaks you. And we are being told in the spiritual timeless instructions that we can access the very power of God to be made strong and enabled to live that life. We are offered that power that allows us to choose to be good when we don't feel like it – to sacrifice, to make the extra effort – to keep our mouth shut when it needs to be shut – all those things that are oh so human.

We can't do this all by ourselves. We're fragile, mortal, selfish people. But if we are made strong with the power of his mighty strength, then we are channeling Holy Spirit indwelling within us. That's a mighty destiny. That's a transforming destiny. That allowed you to live and die in peace and joy.

And may you be prepared to endure everything with patience. Not only must we learn to endure with patience, which in itself a gigantic effort, he says, *"while joyfully giving thanks to the Father."* In other words, we are actually told – sacred instructions now – that we must learn to be happy and joyful when everything is wrong. Think about it. That is about as untypical as you can get. Our whole world is about not feeling that way. It's raining on my parade – I've got all this to complain about. It's too cold for me - like the universe did something against you or something. We are called to this unique genius teaching – that it is possible to be happy when there is no reason to be happy. Can you imagine what that would do to your life? Can you imagine what kind of human being you would become? There are such people who despite all the trials and tribulations of life, all the defeats, all the injustices, and death itself are joyful. My friends in Europe call it "the sacrifice of joy." It is actually a spiritual discipline to be happy in spite of because then you are truly dying to the old ways and living for the new ways. And it changes everything.

Think of the last time you were at the doctors or someplace with other people – maybe the Bureau of Motor Vehicles – that's a good place, and look at the faces around you. There's a lot of unhappy people. Impatient, unhappy, angry -- it's a list that won't quit. Well, let me remind you that in this teaching, if you peek at Colossians 3, we are given a list of those kinds of instructions I was talking about, instructions that are specific to our lives and call us to not just be any old way.

Hear this now – you've heard it before. The question is have you lived it? "But now you must rid yourself," that's pretty plain isn't it? "of all such things as these: anger, rage, malice, slander, filthy language from your lips. You have taken off your old self with its practices and put on the new." This is serious business. This is spiritual discipline, spiritual warfare and every one of us is called to it. None of us have any excuses. And please understand, it doesn't mean don't judge and condemn yourself if you slip because everybody's going to slip, but if we're all trying for the same thing, we'll help each other out. We'll be able to forgive each other, to all understand that we're in the same boat, and to rise together to a state that is closer to what we are called to be. That is what church is about.

He goes on to say that He is the image of the invisible God. Incredible. The fullness of God was pleased to dwell in Jim. People don't quite know what to do with that. You've got your academics saying, "Well I've got a low Christology," and that sort of thing. The point is Jesus of Nazareth in His way of being, in His forgiveness of evil while confronting it, in His forgiveness of the worst sins in order for them to go and sin no more is the prototype of what every human being should be.

This is the God-given example of who you are meant to be. I've quoted Luther this morning because sometimes it helps to hear from a familiar figure. We are meant to be the hidden mercy of God. Think about that. Imagine yourself as the hidden mercy of God. You seem normal, seem like the average person, but you're full of mercy, ready to help another. The world could use a few of those don't you think?

All of this we hear at the end was to reconcile the world to Himself by making peace through the blood of the cross. That is so full of Jewish background metaphor – of Paul's way of talking. Here's what I have to say to you about that because it is such a travesty. The God of unconditional love did not need a blood sacrifice in order to reconcile us to Himself. The blood of the cross is the decision that Jesus makes to go all the way into our human suffering and to all the injustices we endure that we might know the Divine is with us.

That blood is sacrificial love for your redemption. It isn't magic. It isn't satisfying a primitive god. It is showing total self-giving, total letting God through human form, so that He can say, "Forgive them for they know not what they do." And that is what we are meant to be. That is what we are after. That is the way we are to follow, one step at a time. It can be done; it has been done; it will be done. Let us be the ones now, in this time and place, to live these teachings – this Divine wisdom that makes us Christ like, makes us God pleasing, makes us alive and well in the light of God.

6

The Double Life

(Translated from the writings of Father Alphonse and Rachel Goettmann)

I share with you some exceptional teaching coming out
of this quarterly journal *Le Chemin* which is published by
The Community of Bethanie in Eastern France headed
by Father Alphonse and his wife Rachel Goettmann
whose books my wife and I translated, and whom I
consider among the highest spiritual teachers alive today.
Their experiential knowledge, consciousness, scholarship
regarding the Source of spiritual teachings buried deep
within Christianity, is unsurpassed. In this particular
issue, available only in French, there is an exceptional
article followed by just a few lines of the basics and
fundamentals of the spiritual life. As you read these

radiant words, try to digest them slowly and stop when a word or phrase resonates particularly strongly for you. Let it sink in.

The most important point is to not have a double life. On one side the family, job, pleasures, the other side prayer and worship. We are disciples full time and all the time. Our vocation unifies us completely. There is a convergence, a fusion – a living fusion of all that we do throughout the day right unto the least detail towards that unique source Jesus the Christ. The only ideal of the disciple is complete identification with Christ. The means of working toward this union was this rooting into Christ are essentially the following:

1) Before anything else, one and only a unique effort – what we might call the effort to live, to be Christ in all and each moment to let Him live in me, through me – whatever I am doing, whatever I am thinking, speaking, actions, and suffering – it is He who does it in me, for me. Our efforts are generally multiple and limited – multiple as such they divide us; we break our head against their psychic complications. Limited because they are applied at particular points of our lives and leave all the rest of life aside. To replace all this with one single effort, to be Christ in all is obviously to place oneself at the center point of all transformation of self and of action in the external world. It is also to discover what extent all is suddenly simple and extremely liberating – blossoming. Everything is easy, fertile, carried to a new level of existence. The most important will be perseverance – to begin again each and every day without quitting, without ever being worn out. There is the secret of the method. There is no other. Soon the Christ will be for us a reality that is a stunning consistence – *"the one that we have heard, touched, seen"* – quoting First John.

2) To frequent the sacred writings every day to enter into a familiarity with the Christ, not to read, but to meditate the texts, to digest them as the ancients said, even if it's only one sentence a day. It is never a question of quantity.

3) The clear look upon oneself for the examination of conscience confronts us continually with the Master.

71

Always at night to look over one's day and foresee tomorrow. Why did I progress or fall today; how did I do that? What can I do tomorrow to take one step further?

4) The body is here an extraordinary help. We are in the tradition of incarnation. Christ is my flesh and my blood and my breath. To feel his presence agrees within me, nut this presupposes that my being is completely devoted to this. Certain spiritual masters prescribe exercises on this that are very precise to tune the body towards this, making of it a bridge toward the beyond.

These words whether you are a Christian or not speak a truth that is ultimate that is utterly transformational. You can see its parallels in many teachings. It is very important that in trying to absorb what is given to you here that we're not speaking of Jesus of Nazareth with the beard and the sandals, but of that Christ consciousness, that connection, that access to the Uncreated, that connection between the temporal and the eternal that has been made available to us through this particular pathway, this particular incarnation, this particular holy man.

So think through these steps, what they are - straightforward, simple. You can see how they connect with the work. You can see that to do a little here and a little there rather than holistic, complete dedication to a unique aim is indeed the key, so I offer this to you – this spontaneous translation for your reflections given to us by one who has truly reached a higher level of light and consciousness and I hope that for yourself, you begin to experience what that might be.

7

The Awakened State

We are gifted once again with a very interesting question fundamental to this whole effort of spiritual awakening - whatever tradition you have come from or studied. All of them, those who are authentic, lead to this blossoming into a higher consciousness. And our member gives us his own specific experience writing, as he says, literally just moments after having come out of a state of sleep – sleep state – or first state (to speak in the Fourth Way vernacular) and wants to share with us some thoughts and questions about this. So, this should be very common to all of you wallowing in thoughts depression, self-pity, etc.

I describe them as a constant companion, hovering like a dark cloud – a wonderful metaphor because it is indeed a dark cloud. You can see it in people – the trick is to see it in ourselves because that dark cloud is the opposite of the radiant joy which is the sign of someone who has authentically connected with Spirit, encountered the reality of the living God, and entered into a so transcendent place. And then he tells us that after reading – it happens to be one of the books that my wife and I translated *"The Beyond Within"* by Father Alphonse Goettmann and his wife Rachel, who you should know by now, are great living saints among us - he made that effort to pick up and read, which oddly enough, as I mention it are the very words that came to St. Augustine who had the greatest influence on western Christianity for a thousand years is transition from Manichean, Pagan way of thinking to Christian, began with that voice, *"Pick up and read."*

In fact, I believe that he heard children singing in a game and he picked up a Bible and opened it and that was the beginning - that was the shock that sent him into a new consciousness. So, our friend here in his parallel way made that effort to start something and that is a teaching right there. When you know you're in a place you don't want to be in, find your own ways to come out of it. Gurdjieff speaks of alarm clocks to wake us up – "enabling factors" he calls them. Find something beautiful; step outside – do what you need to do. What you don't want to do is linger in that dark cloud of whatever it is that has become a familiar companion and pattern and that we have become addicted to, and in many ways think of as "ourselves." So the critical turning point early on is to recognize that these old habits, emotional habits are faulty, poisonous, and deadly. They will steal your life from you. So, do not allow yourself to wallow in them.

If you are brutally honest with yourself, you will recognize that some folks find perverse pleasure in melancholia, anger, depression, and self-pity. All that has to be dealt with – with a certain mercilessness. In fact, the great teachers early on at the Source of all Faith say, "Have no self-pity. Do not allow self-pity into your life," It's critical – that is the kind of spiritual self-discipline that it takes to walk this path. There are no excuses –

even when life is terrible and I speak to you from experience, not only for myself, but for individuals – I can think of three or four right now that I dealt with today – who are in very difficult circumstances, are not studying esoteric teachings, and yet have the inner strength to find peace and hope and to keep going. We must at least be that strong if we are serious about this. So, he makes the effort to read and something happens. "I just had this awakening feeling come over me and not only an awakening, but it immediately tied to a previous time of awakening. This is what is known technically, if you will, as the third state of consciousness. The second state being the awakening state – which is waking sleep – the first state being actually sleeping. This third state also being self-remembering. So this higher state, this awakened state is what that mysterious term [foreign] the remembrance of the self is all about. And it is so vivid, so different, that he can't even remember the last time it happened.

Ouspensky speaks about this saying that it is only those high points of third states on consciousness that we truly remember and you can verify that for yourself in your own life. He can report these dates because that is how substantial these moments are. And that is truly the case. The immensity of peace or contentment or gratitude or joy that floods you changes you completely – and your circumstances. We all have the birthright to know this. And so he goes on, "and my question is, what is the best way to remain in this state as long as possible?" And these, of course, are key advanced questions. Advanced, I say, because we have to have made personal efforts – that of self-observation, of divided attention, of not being what we have been, of seeing what the wrong work that is interfering – all of that which most of the world has no interest in and that evil will fight to the death against. For those of you who are moving forward, for whom this is great significance, then these questions become not theoretical or intellectual, but very real – life and death.

What is the best way to stay in this state as long as possible? My answer to you is that one develops a sensitivity to this higher energy because it is when we find energy that is circulating in your being, in your body and your receptivity toward it can let it last longer. In fact, our natural reaction to this higher energy, which is potent and strong is to release it because can instinctively can hardly handle it. That is why people applaud – release that emotional energy – jump up and down – all those things that instead of containing it and keeping it directed and intentional, one is trying to get rid of it. I try in various ways to help the folks in our congregation to sustain a place they may have found prayer for as long as they can. A prayer state does not end with opening your eyes. Move on; it is so easy to lose it. We're so distractible; we're so unaware of the significance of it. So you must treasure it like the pearl of great price. You must recognize what is happening enough to give it as much space as possible and not allow anything from within or without to take it away because it will go away. It is possible for these states to last for hours.

We have written evidence that Blaise Pascal, seventeenth century French scientist/mystic wrote specifically about his state. You'll find this in his famous *Pensées* (Thoughts) written long ago. This brilliant, rational man discovered this higher state – that moment – tears of joy – he could hardly find the words for it and it lasted for a long time.

We are not here to seek exotic experiences but to be more and more transparent to the divine, as so many say -- such as John of the Cross -- and to be a dwelling place of Holy Spirit so that it is a matter of a use of attention that remains receptive, that remains connected, that slowly but surely expands in these states. The second part of the question is are these moments only fleeting moments of God's grace that pass, or can they be kept up for times indefinite? The truth is that grace has much to do with it of course. We cannot manufacture it, but we sure can lay the groundwork for it as I've told you so many times. Unless we're hit over the head once in a while, like Paul falling off his horse in Damascus, most of the time it is a combination, a co-creation – it is the unexpected results of continued effort and work and dedication to becoming that receptive cup. The ancients speak of grace-filled people so that it is not grace coming and going – it is there.

There are holy people, saints and others – sages who sustain it for very long durations of time, who develop a unity within and a consistency of lifestyle of being where there is no room for fragmentation and contradiction.

81

This leads us to the next question – *"For those who have been in the work, can they stay in this state all the time or do you just experience them more frequently for longer durations?"* Clearly the evolution of this octave of awakening means more frequent experiences of higher consciousness, and of longer duration. Once we begin to taste how precious these states are, the more we want them. No question about it – that alone will let you know you have touched on something of the true mystical awakening. And you will want more; you will hunger for more. You will not want negativity to come back and pull you down into the basement of yourself, poison your day or have your peace stolen from you. You begin to really dedicate yourself to a unique desire, which is living in that consciousness. That is the aim; that is the direction ultimately.

It does become more frequent; you may be sure of that. One is less identified with everything. Worry, anxiety, and fear dissipate because the reality of the living one is palpable and ever-present and impacts our daily life. That's not to say that accompanied with that is more hardships sometimes because it appears that there is a parallel sometimes between more hardship and advancing on the way. Sorry to bring you the news. At the same time, the hardship strengthens the inner spirit and the stretching of ourselves in sacrificial care and other ways of living in the world bring the promise and the reward – the opportunity to give more and more, dying to self and living more in this consciousness.

The idea of living in it all the time belongs to the highest, most developed among us, and there are such people among us, but there does come a time when the authentic, spiritual seeker – the one who has found the way, not still seeking everywhere else – realizes that there is no other way to live. That may require moving away from certain ways of being and individuals who will interfere with that – turning off horror movies – a great variety of things – that then allow everything to contribute to a gentility and sensitivity in which this higher energy can habitate. We must be the habitat; we must empty ourselves to be filled. And the culture does everything it can to do the opposite. We have to get our nose out of watching the news sometimes because all that happens there is we react to what we hear or see.

That's in its practical ways, how we move more and more into frequent states.

But it is a certain kind of death because we are less concerned with our basic needs, our worries for survival, and more in tune with the moment, with that which is not visible and be present with spiritual eyes on the reality around us. Finally he states an observation is that, "While I was in a state of sleep, I knew I was in a state of sleep, but I could not get out no matter how much I wrestled." He speaks of terrible thoughts and so forth, "All I can hope is that it stays away but judging by my previous experiences, I would eventually sleep again." You may be sure of that. We all continually struggle with stumbling back. Of that, there is no question, but each time that we fall into that sleep we are more perceptive. As that occurs, then we can do the kind of work that prepares us for attracting to ourselves and invoking within our minds that which is holy, that which is vaster, that which is the joy that no one can take away. That is awakening. May you find it, taste it – see that that is your true home.

PART TWO

"Christian is one who lives in accordance with Christ's precepts. Such as we are we cannot be Christians. In order to be Christians we must be able 'to do.' We cannot do; with us everything 'happens."

G.I. Gurdjieff

8

The Fourth Way and Christian Teaching

On your spiritual journey, you may have come across in your own readings books on The Fourth Way Books and Mystical Christianity. In these parallel materials there are at times paradoxical statements and contradictions that can be very confusing. So if you look at this question posed by a student, you see that the individual is pointing out what he is using a certain fundamentalism approach for understanding the Fourth Way, which he defines as intolerant of anyone outside the "in group." He quotes Ouspensky, whom you may know was the first primary student of Gurdjieff and wrote *In Search of the Miraculous*. He eventually broke away from Gurdjieff and taught in England for many years. He had a thousand students and from his group came Maurice Nicoll who, in my view, is the finest expression of what Gurdjieff tried to bring to the western world. But he is saying that Ouspensky is quoted as saying, "Those who did not do the "Work" [the inner work of awakening] which is designed to create a soul – or higher consciousness – would "die like dogs." That is not a particularly enlightened position.

So his question is: *How to reconcile this attitude with the Christian calling?* This is where we – as we open ourselves to learn new things -- discover that we fail to employ the Socratic method of recognizing how little we know. Oddly enough, the perennial teaching "Know Thyself" (inscribed on the Temple of Delphi) means precisely that we must find out how much you don't know. The fact is that we must trust our deepest intuitions which are rooted in Holy Spirit, in the energies of God, the state of higher consciousness which connect us with something greater than ourselves. We are that drop in the ocean which contains the entire ocean as Rumi states, so we can trust something within us beyond the petty ego and the pathologies that everyone has and which distort our sense of self. It is correct to say that it is not a very enlightened position to say that everyone will die like dogs if they don't do this inner work which the Fourth Way makes available. This is certainly not a Christian view. We know, in fact, that Christ specifically sought out people who were going to die like dogs, who were lost, who were adulterers, who were desecrating their own existence — in order to waken them to that greater reality.

So, the unenlightenedness of that statement should send up red flags. Wherever you find intolerance, something should tell you deep within your gut — the center of your being — that this is not right. You can guess all the different ways that fundamentalist Christianity deviated from Truth because of its intolerance. But some of you also, no doubt, know that, from the sixties on, we've had gurus, teachers, and esoteric groups that have created their own little subculture and almost without exception among their criteria you will find a rejection and dislike of those who are not one of them. That is, of course, the definition of a cult. In the esoteric school in which I studied, and which was highly sophisticated with very educated people, none of us realized that there were dynamics created as this community evolved (or devolved) which were cult-like. I have mentioned previously that teacher in that school would call everyone out there who was not working on themselves "life people" with an obvious sense of superiority. This is a clear contradiction to the deep and universal Truth which insists humility is key to spiritual awakening.

It is critical that in studying these ideas, they must be parallel with the deepest ideas of Truth found in the teachings of the Christ. If you have rejected Christianity because of negative experiences, be sure to not mistake the vessel for the cargo as Gurdjieff would say. The heart of Christianity, going back to the earliest times, carries with it a dynamic spirit of transformational, unconditional love. Period. It's what you see when you see Mother Theresa, John of the Cross, Theresa of Avila, Thomas Merton and so many more, who in their humility are beautiful beings.

Therefore, approach these psychological teachings of the Fourth Way with the knowledge that they must end up being a contribution to your becoming a good person --

and that means one who does not reject, one who does not consider himself better than another. We must face the fact that Ouspensky and Gurdjieff certainly had their human foibles. It is clear that 65 years after Gurdjieff's death in 1949 certain schools idolize him to such an extent that they have made the terrible mistake of confusing the messenger for the Message.

Gurdjieff had his flaws. He was not the Anointed One, the Christ. Ouspensky would spend his evenings according to those who were close to him, drinking his vodka late into the night and being very melancholic. So something was missed, and that's why, for myself, I've studied for these thirty-five years, it was very much tied up in conjunction with the mystics, not only from other religions, but back home in Christianity. We have hardly scratched the surface of that legacy. Most Christians don't know Theophan the Recluse or any of the great teachers or saints of ancient Christianity who gave us a psychotherapy that is timeless, a methodology that is sometimes difficult to grasp in reading their works which is why the Fourth Way is useful. You can understand, "Do not identify." In other words, do not let yourself get pulled out of yourself and become the object that you see in front of you, caught up and therefore full of anger and so forth. Remember always that the goal of awakening, of self-awareness, of living in a higher consciousness is always about the very same thing that Christ brought into the world which is unconditional, agape love.

For those of you who haven't seen it, my spiritual message on the parable of the prodigal son, is worth considering because that is the classic, ultimate paradigm, which Jesus expresses like no one else has ever expressed – paints a picture of the nature of the Uncreated One and our relationship to that reality and its transformational impact on us.

So trust your deepest instincts spiritually when you find something like we have before us and recognize that even a great philosopher like Ouspensky had his limitations and flaws. We are not out to make any assumptions that they had everything right. Each of us in our own individual way has to find that which is truest for themselves and match it with the greatest teachings, the summit of human understanding which is that which the Christ brought to us when it is lived out in our midst and made into our own transformation and identity. The heat of the battle is in the moment. The effortless effort of being present of not being stressed out and caught up in the unreality of our minds and imagination – this is great power, but you must discern and walk that narrow path.

9

False Personality

We deal here with the specifics of doing this inner work and it is when we get to these specifics that real opportunities for change takes place. We get past general ideas, philosophizing, comparative religion and all that down to the essence of what these ideas, these teachings, these instructions are really meant to do. A member speaks of something that you may have experienced, "I've noticed that I have to speak my false Personality in order to observe it. For example, I'm not feeling fear at the moment, but I say something that shows fear, that reveals fear." That's a very valuable insight because the first grounding or foundational work for us for authentic awakening is to see, is to observe objectively. Now what is within us? And at the beginning, it can only be seen as it comes out. We are not expected to be able to flip a switch and be a different person. We have to see who we are as we are now. And therefore, if you'll recall at the beginning, it was highly emphasized not to judge yourself and not to critique it, not to consider it a failure, but just to be able to have the objective will and honesty about oneself to see it for what it is – to be willing to be vulnerable enough for the sake of your True Self to see what is false, what is negative, what is pathological, what is unnecessary, and to recognize it as it happens.

It is not expected that we can clean the inside of the cup as Christ says, without first knowing what's in it. And so allow yourself to just see and the more you are able to capture images of yourself objectively, the more you will clearly understand what the meaning of false personality is, features, etcetera. The member goes on to say, "I could not be able to notice it unless the words came out of my mouth." That is true. We are certainly not dealing with conceptual thinking, we are dealing with organic experience and sometimes it's in our worst moments that we can see most clearly what our problems are. By problems, I mean obstacles to higher consciousness. She goes on to say that, "Other times I catch myself saying something and then I can't stop saying what I was saying because I have no power to stop it even while observing it. What do I do in those cases?" No power to stop it while observing it - the day will come when you will have the power to stop it. But this is the great work. The ancients called it the Royal Road – the Royal Way. It's a secret mystery of mysteries because it is the spiritual evolution of human beings. So, when you witness it and witness your inability to stop it, you are simply gaining information – authenticating, verifying what the work teaches about us and or stimulus response function, and the way you will get to the point of having the power to stop it.

It's the development of a greater and greater dislike for that behavior – for the taste of it, for the poison of it, for what it does to you and others – to your life, to your everyday life. And the day will eventually come when there will be enough inner separation that you know this is no longer you functioning. It is no longer how you wish to respond to the world and you will have that split second space, psychological space in which you can choose to not only stop the behavior, but to transform it through understanding and take that energy that was going to be wasted, lost and alchemically change it into awareness – pure awareness, self-awareness, awareness of the other which ultimately leads to purification and power of compassion.

So, to work with those energies and know that they can go into the dark or into the light and that we are the crossroads is key and the day does come when you suddenly are able to not be that and to become more and to see differently, to discover another perspective, another way of dealing with people to connect with a deeper source and to understand that living in that place of the true self, of the higher consciousness of disentangling yourself from old ways connects you to something eternal, something entirely fulfilling, peacemaking, enabling you to become all that you can be – the potential that your divine self, your maker has always wanted from you. It is available; it's why we're given willpower. Use it rightly. So don't be discouraged –

ever – because each step, each difficulty leads to that place where you can begin the transformation process.

10

Self-Remembering

This strange term that is used in the Fourth Way was created by Gurdjieff and named self-remembering, or the Third State of Consciousness. A student asks, "What are some concrete examples of how someone can experience self-remembering in daily life and is it similar to the remembrance of God"?

If you've been looking through the materials,[1] you may have found that a parallel term to this reference to a state of consciousness that is mysterious to us – you know how difficult it is to categorize such things – another term for self-remembering is the third state of consciousness. What does this mean? Perhaps by

---

[1] The materials referenced here are available at http://innerworkforspiritualawakening.com/.

approaching it this way you will understand more of what the term implies and how you can recognize it in daily life. In these teachings, the first state of consciousness is that of literally being asleep in bed. It's as simple as that. The second state of consciousness is also known as waking sleep and this is our way of being in daily life as we are – what we take for granted. We assume we are conscious and that is where the great mistake is. We are functioning on automatic, we are seemingly present to our lives and would swear we are in fact conscious when indeed without that inner awareness, we are operating in that semi state of sleep where imagination and false assumptions and misperceptions and illusions about ourselves – all those wrong work, if you will, those elements of wrong work complicate our lives and make them what they are.

The third state of consciousness is therefore something different than what we normally experience as living the moment of our daily lives. We have all had experiences of what Gurdjieff calls self-remembering - in French *le rapel de soi* or "the remembering of one's self" and you can recognize these moments because they create a special memory in your lives – moments in your past that stand out and they can be moments of profound peace on a beach, on a mountaintop – some transcendent moment of serenity that takes over for a brief moment – brings that contentment and fulfillment, wholeness, plentitude is one word for it – that is so precious and is truly what we all yearn for consciously and unconsciously in our existence. Such moments occur also in times of great danger when we are suddenly in a state of extreme vigilance because of a situation that has heightened our senses and we are extremely present to our surroundings to our moment, all of the chaos inside as cleared and we are in fact in a moment of consciousness that is sharpened, heightened, vivid.

We also have such moments of self-remembering, third state of consciousness as instances of grace in the midst of a very difficult situation, of a tragedy, of a great stress – suddenly peace fills us inexplicably – nothing we have done and in spite of all that we are dealing with, all the complications we enter an inner sanctuary – calm. That may happen in a moment of crisis when something within us is called forth.

103

Again, it is an expansion of consciousness beyond ourselves, beyond our pettiness. It is a state of, a surfacing of a deeper self that is not caught up in the vanity of life, the taking of offense, the worries and so forth. So they are truly remarkable moments and they can go all the way back to earliest childhood. Moments of beauty – witnessing, standing before a great painting – all of those kinds of high moments that we cannot generally recognize as special. We cannot name them and yet they stay with us because they have such power.

It is said that looking back upon our lives those greatest memories, those high moments are in fact those moments of the remembering of self. It is asked here, "Is it a similar to the remembrance of God?" and the answer is absolutely. But it is a paradox, here we speak of remembering oneself – this presence to oneself and one's life taking us out of the mundane into a taste of the eternal in time if you will, a taste of the self we have always been from childhood to old age present – not to complicate matters, but sometimes called the time body – some quality of ourselves that is who we've always been despite the shifting chapters and roles we've played throughout our lives.

That self we know intimately – that little child – that spirit within. But those moments cannot be manufactured; there is mystery in them and that paradox I just mentioned has to do with the fact that entering that greater state of self, we in fact leave self (what we think is self our personality and so forth) and indeed enter that holiness of remembrance of something greater than ourselves. Perhaps you had that moment entering a cathedral or something of that nature.

We know these states, we just haven't valued them, haven't realized that is the purpose of our existence, that is the goal – to live there, to be that, to mature into that, to awaken to that event horizon if you will, of being that which makes us more noble creatures, that blossoms on potential in ways beyond our greatest hope. So the work itself is to prepare the ground for those moments, to maximize the possibility of their occurring.

If we begin our day in that waking sleep, second state of consciousness, in a bad mood, one thing after another as you may have read in some of the materials. You spill your coffee, you stub your toe, and the momentum begins. You're impatient in traffic, you shut yourself out, and you minimize the possibility of the grace-filled moment that gives meaning to your existence. So the inner work of cleansing, of unifying, of not being identified, which is a critical term you'll be studying, in which we are both hypnotized and pulled out of ourselves by the events of life, sold out if you will, to the things of this world, remain just stimulus-response mechanisms. That is what that word means.

When we are in that state of identification we are lost to that deeper self, which is why divided attention, inner separation, non-identifying, recognizing through self-observation, the negativity, the wrong work, the rigid habits, illusions are all about clearing the way for the purity and beauty of what is named here in technical terms as self-remembering.

So we play a role in that – very much so because the more we make those moment-by-moment efforts - those little efforts, the more we are capable, potentially of receiving these higher states of consciousness and they begin to occur more often and we hunger for them more and we value them more and so we make room for them, and yes indeed, as has been said, the goal is that they become more and more frequent. This is the Pearl of Great Price. Living in the presence of God to use another terminology, in which we are lifted up, lifted out of all that mundaneness of the little self and commune with a vaster understanding of reality, of our identity, of the glory of being alive in the moment. These are complex issues and yet infinitely simple because they are our natural habitat, our spiritual – we go against our nature which is self-absorbed and self-interested and fighting against others for whatever we are after, but it is our birthright to live in those times of pure joy and peace, which is resurrection, which is awareness of our purpose. Peace in the sight of holy, confidence in what is fully present in the moment where we encounter something of the eternal.

11

Secret Union with God

(Translation from Father Alphonse and Rachel Goettmann)

I propose today to share with you another translation from the original French of a letter coming to us from the community Bethanie in eastern France written by Father Alphonse Goettmann and his radiant wife Rachel, whose books have touched the lives of thousands of people across Europe with their profound depths of spiritual wisdom. So I share with you a very special teaching that reveals the experiential dimension the liturgy and rituals of the Eastern Orthodox Church:

At the first creation, God placed within the human being a unique desire for the unique desired one that God is, but cut off from God in the fall, the human being seeks to satisfy that desire someplace else. Our desire fragments itself into the multiple and seeks in countless ways in that world of the relative, a response to its thirst for the absolute. That is why desire is the powerful symbol of our self and the true barometer of our spiritual life as long as we are not centered on God alone, the desire or desire is the enemy par excellence of the path, of the way, of the spiritual journey. It requires an extreme vigilance to discover it under all its hidden ways and disguises and to constantly be on watch for those obscure satisfactions and pleasures when someone has lost God they experience a permanent state of lack.

Bur for the one who has understood through experience that in the depths each desire – of every desire, even the least of them there is in truth the desire for God. Then that person can become poor of all the rest - his or her consciousness turns towards the Divine Presence which is at the heart of this interior thrust, interior energy or urge and no longer aimed towards the objects of our desires.   One day such a person will be possessed by God instead is being processed by things.

In the end the human being, each of us, rediscovers that unique desire that encounters God within all things, even in those satisfactions and pleasures but these now will be places of encounter, of connection with the Holy One and no longer prisons of the ego. Poverty in this person can become absolute. It translates itself concretely in a complete equality of the soul before all results - you might say another way a complete calm of the soul, before all results, before all reactions, all circumstances - if it's good or bad, fortune, respect or insult, fame or blame, victory or defeat, health or illness, happy or tragic circumstances.

Whatever they are, the only thing that counts for such a person is what God wants here and now. Such a person only wants what God wants in every moment and everything that happens to such a person is accepted indifferently from God's hand. The smallest reaction of one's heart in the face of what occurs – the smallest reaction - is proof of a non-poverty and of an attachment to the old nature. This poverty is first of all to become free of everything. For this freedom is the great sign of all personhood. When a human being awakens to this freedom he or she is born to themselves, to their true mystery, to their identity. This is an immense letting go, a leap into a complete and total confidence where another than the Ego becomes the guide, the conductor of everything because desire rests only in God. All this can be said very easily when in fact it is the battle of a lifetime but the path can be quick for one who has decided to go that way and pays the price. Amateurism in this area is a dead end. Only the one who exercises themselves with relentlessness can move forward on this path.

Yet even then one must be very careful because that unique desire can hide a will to power, a pride however subtle that such a person is spiritual, that the search for the accomplishment, the fulfillment of self is still at hand even in the presence of God. The self must disappear. After one's attachment to things, we are ourselves our own wealth. We are still a source of that desire which seems legitimate in our lives – the desire for God and therefore we feel ourselves alive. Yet we must die to self completely if not, nothing will take place. Even a self that is hungry for God is still egocentric. That self still has its autonomy and continues to live in its kingdom of desire. For the egotistical desire there can be no accomplishment, no fulfillment. Liberation or salvation can only be found in losing oneself. God does not come along with other things, not even our own self as long as there is a self, there is now room for a You (capital Y). And even if there is room, it would be too much; we would take up too much space. We generally tend to imagine that a human being is empty of self and of all things there would be room watch for God to dwell within and that is a great error, so say the Holy Ones, the Ancient Ones, the early fathers and mothers.

Meister Eckhart, for example, has a profound insight on this in which he describes authentic poverty in this way: the thought, however tiny it may be, however light it is, still presents itself as a "having something." It is a richness, that is to say a filling - fulfillment of desire. If a person is empty of all things, of all creatures, of himself and of God, says Meister Eckhart, and if God could still find room in this person to act, I would say as long as that room exists this person is not poor with a poverty hat is most intimate. We human beings must not have a place but be ourselves the place in which God acts. And that is what God would enjoy doing. It is here in that poverty that man recovers eternal being - that eternal being that we once were, that we are now, and that we will be forever. We therefore must not possess or hold on to anything, not even a self that allows the reception pf God's visitation, not even an absence of self which is still a possible object of pride.

The similarity between God and the human being then becomes complete. We are one with God, identified with God and from that point on we no longer know a separate self. We have found our true self because it is lost in God. Holy wisdom friends for this holy time.

12

The Wolf and the Lamb Metaphor

Friends, this is a very straightforward metaphor: the wolf and the lamb within. The lamb representing our essence, the gentility of spirit, the hunger for spirituality and the wolf representing the instinctive animal part of our nature. Because we have begun to observe hopefully that we are not one, but a multiplicity – surely the simple division of lamb and wolf is understandable. Perhaps everyone has witnessed what happens when a wolf appears in a friend you thought was a lamb.

The shock is overwhelming because the schizophrenic-like behavior is so intense. Old Robert Louis Stevenson had it right – no doubt connected to an esoteric school of his day in the nineteenth century – there is a Jeckel and Hyde element – surely we all know that. And we must be on alert and to be on alert is precisely the core of the teachings of Yeshua, the Anointed One. Watch, do not sleep. In the gospel of Thomas there's talk about stand at the top of your vineyard and watch for the thief coming in.

We have within us aspects of self that are degenerate, that are violent, and that have no interest in spirituality. We cannot hide that behind an illusion of who we think we are. The work speaks of buffers that separate these compartmentalized identities so that one cannot know the other.

So the warning is that it is serious spiritual warfare and in most cases the wolf wins over the lamb by sheer force of nature, so we are facing off with a powerful enemy if we are on a true spiritual journey. And that wolf can be defined in multiple ways including vanity and pride and those features that will not let go and that will not allow their force to be taken away – their life so that something else can live. Therefore, it is important to acknowledge that reality – to see it when it is happening – to discern from eilakrisis (the spiritual term of the ancient fathers to discern that which is not from God), that which is of God, and that which seeks God and recognize that we have to make choices on whose side we're on. The wolf will make sure, at every turn, to keep you away from the path of the lamb and the path of self-transcendence so that he can live in his own self-satisfaction. This is the great, perennial human battle and we are engaged in something very big, but the results are extraordinary when they work. We must be willing to see the wolf and all that comes with it to declare war on it so that the good and the transcendent and the compassionate can win out. It is a long battle full of pitfalls, but it is *the* battle – the purpose for being here in this world – life as school – existence as spiritual – awakening and evolution. So, know yourself well enough to recognize that wolf and to have the courage to confront it for the sake of the good.

Many are familiar with the famous Cherokee Indian wisdom saying of the grandfather teaching to his grandson about the two wolves who live inside, one good – one bad, battling each other and the grandson asks who wins. That famous wisdom is universal and perennial: the one you feed is the one who wins. Indeed, that is a truth which one can reflect on for a lifetime.

A student has made the point that there is a subtlety in the statement made from the quote out of *Meetings With Remarkable Men*: "Can you find the force to enable these two quite opposite lives to live together in yourself?" The assumption is that the wolf and the lamb, these metaphors of our psychologies -- spiritual/ animal, gentle/ violent -- are meant to somehow co-exist. We all must face the fact that to the end of our days there will be some form of duality within us with which we will all have to struggle.

Let me put at rest a mistake that could be made here – one easily made in a Gurdjieffian context because he so often liked to "step on our corns" as he said, to confuse and to push, to force us to think for ourselves. It is clear in the mysticism of the Christian teaching, both East and West, that we are not meant to coexist as these two shockingly different beings. We must recognize, as Paul says so famously in Romans 8: "*I do the things that I do not*

wish to do." What is it in me that causes me to do this?"
This psychoanalysis from the first century is something
with which we are all too familiar. That is why the great
teachers of early Christianity, these athletes of the Spirit,
are so important to us – especially for those of us in the
Western world who have not known such models of
transformation. We must indeed face off and crush that
within which is the enemy, which is darkness, which is
ungodly, even if we know that we will not ever be fully
free.

Consider that great metaphorical story of Christ in the
wilderness. In the gospel of Luke it ends with the devil
(the wolf) waiting to return for another time! So even
with the greatest Master, there is this continued assault.
As they say, the wolf is always at the door.

Another similar teaching tells us that the lion is always
roaming about seeking whom it may devour. These
painful truths reflect our humanity, our capacity for
horrific violence. Our spiritual efforts are all aimed at
reducing the force out of that dark part of ourselves.
First we must face it, see it, know it, which in itself is

advanced spiritual understanding because most people are completely asleep to themselves and think that they are just wonderful. They believe that everyone else is the problem. They live in an illusion of denial that will not see the other aspects of themselves. These "buffers" manage to blind us to these other selves and so they do not know each other.

"Know thyself" -- That is brutal for everyone because the ego does not want to be seen for what it is and we are prone to either want to love ourselves like little gods or hate ourselves, which is just the opposite of the same thing, and we are guided constantly by those unfortunate features of vanity and pride which keep us away from our center, from our spiritual selves. So inner work is meant to reduce the force of this darkness because as long as we allow that which is ultimately violence to control us, we will not evolve spiritually. We will not awaken.

Saint Francis, that great and very human image of one who became Christ-like, a person of love and light, went to the crusades before he became the saint that we know today, which means that he was blood-soaked and did and saw things that are unspeakable. Upon his return, he threw everything away. We have to make such efforts, at least psychologically, and not allow our multiplicity and weakness of will to keep us double- minded as the letter of James states. A double-minded person can never achieve anything.

So part of this great discipline is to become single-minded and that is a "super-effort" and should not surprise anyone. When one authentically sacrifices for another – in an act of self-transcendence – our heart opens and empowers us. To bless is to become blessed. One of my great turning points is that scene from Victor Hugo's "Les Miserables" featuring the bitter, hateful, broken Jean Valjean. Rejected by all now that he is freed from nineteen years of unjust imprisonment, he is given shelter by this good man who happens to be a priest. The convict, in spite of the kindness shown to him, steals the silver, gets caught, and brought back, and this time he is going down for good. The priest's response, to the shock of the policeman is: "My friend, you forgot the candlesticks." He adds the silver candlesticks to the bag of stolen silver and the policeman let him go. The man weeps like a baby in the sight of such redemptive mercy and he becomes a new and good man.

That is a spiritual path. There are people like the kind priest in this world, people who have been set ablaze with a transcendent love, whose wolf has been tamed. In the Beatitudes, "blessed are the meek" means in Greek: "Blessed are those who can hold great power under control." That is what the word meek means. So, even though we have an animal nature, we can get control, we can overcome. There must be victory. There must be a standing firm that becomes immoveable. This is the lesson throughout history of the people of light. Therefore, we must not be giving ourselves excuses to get away with wrong behavior because we are human, claiming that we don't have the willpower to do it. We do have that power. It is our birthright. It is our true nature. The Work helps us in dismantling personality, in recognizing the dangers of negativity, bringing us into a place that is authentically spiritual, a dwelling place for Holy Spirit.

This is our true destiny, our true hope for happiness. It is not theology nor creed; it is experiential transformation available to you if you make that choice for a lifetime and engage in that spiritual warfare. The ancient fathers teach us to be merciless on ourselves while being full of mercy toward others -- Merciless towards that wolf within.

An ancient story tells of a king who had heard of this Moses character – known to be a magnificent wise man beaming with goodness. He sent his best artists to paint a portrait of this rare man. The portrait was brought back to the king and he beckoned his wise men who understood morphology and psychology even in those ancient days. They could only see a man who was violent by nature, who was a negative creature. That is what the portrait revealed. That is what his nature had been. But Moses had overcome that nature. This story tells us that this is our duty as well – to overcome our nature. Know that you must fight, not out there, but within, and discover the miracle of real transformation.

13

The Heart Center

Let me reference this vocabulary from the Fourth Way: *the Higher Emotional Center*. That's a bit metaphysical and mysterious to most of you no doubt, but it is significant because it suggests at least that beyond our emotions, which we all know about, there is a spectrum – degrees shall we say – a ladder upwards to a whole different kind of use of our emotions.

Let me say first of all that in the Fourth Way, in the work, it is recognized that the emotional center, that part of us that is feeling response – sentiment, intuition, empathy and all of that is, as I've said once before, but perhaps you've missed it, this emotional center is an instrument of knowing. Now let that penetrate. That

125

which we have taken as sentimentality, as anger, or happiness or ecstasy – whatever – is actually an instrument ok knowing. We know things emotionally through the emotional center, which the mind, the intellect cannot know. This is why those who are – whose center of gravity – who live more out of that – tend to be more empathetic, more understanding, more aware of another person's condition. One of my great friends, a Serbian Mystic, that I've spoken of and whose biography has just been released again ("God Entered My Life") would constantly go up to people with his eyes closed no less, and know exactly – reveal to them what their state of soul, of mind, of spirit was and give them something that would lift them up. I have heard dozens and dozens of – up until even last week (although he's been gone for fourteen years) – so many examples of these people having amazing experiences with this man who made no big deal out of this sort of clairvoyant gift out of his heart center that could read people.

I'll give you a strange example from long ago. A friend told me that he came up to Charles in their Orthodox Church with a big, giant smile and said, "Hello Charles, how are you?" Charles looked at him in this case and says, "Oh, you poor man," because he could see right past the smile, right past the words, the act, the acting to the real condition of the person. So, the emotional center, the heart center, is of critical importance. In fact, what the work will tell you – at least the oral tradition (which is very hard to find in writing, which is why I'm sharing this with you) – the oral tradition will tell you that King of Hearts, the intellectual part of the emotional center, that is to say that the level of emotion – the refinement of emotion that is present when we listen to beautiful music, when we go to museums and so forth – that more refined use of emotion as opposed to yelling at a football game – the King of Hearts – the intellectual part of the emotional center is the gateway to Higher Centers.

It is through this quality of refined emotion, of intelligent emotion, that we make contact with yet a whole new level of knowing, perceiving, and understanding higher centers, which do not operate automatically, but they are always there accessible. We just don't rise up out of the basement of ourselves to be in touch with them. Now, this is a language that is very specific, you might say technical, but it is just a means to put words to that which is so difficult to express – which could be expressed in other terms, religious terms - but here is meant to help you grasp in some way the wonderful mystery and wonderful potential we have in our spiritual awakening. So, our friend refers to a higher emotional center that is beyond that gateway – that part of ourselves that we can get to with just a little intentionality – opening onto a quality of knowing that blends with higher consciousness – with remembering of self, with real self – with a presence that connects with The Presence.

From that higher emotional center comes the kind of intuition and awareness that is blessed, that is benediction that is channel of spirit into the world. Each of us must discover for ourselves the taste, the realities of such an experience. It is not something to read about; it is something to become. As one of the teachers Karlfried Dürckheim would say - or for that matter John of the Cross – "becoming transparent to the Divine." This is a whole other vocabulary meaning the same thing. Transparent to that quality of being and knowing where unconditional love is possible. Where forgiveness and loving your enemies is possible. It is not possible in the lower parts of the emotional center – in that which yells at the football game. That's the part of our emotional brain that is going to fight, is going to hate, and is going to resist the other. But as we rise up in awareness, in sensitivity, in knowing how to not just react, but intentionally make choices, intentionally align ourselves with our true potential – then a whole different use of the heart center happens and that is when The Way becomes real for us – when the Christ-like way is possible as template for how every human being should be. So indeed, the heart is at the heart of The Work – of all spiritual work.

14

Dealing with Anger as an Inner Tool

The *Philokalia* is a compilation of spiritual and mystical teachings of the Eastern Church roughly from the fourth to the tenth or eleventh century, often methods and teachings to monks and is considered the most sacred book of that part of Christianity which was the origin of source for that first thousand years before the split with the west.

However, this about a specific psychological reality that has to do with us right now – a paradoxical one as most of you know, spirituality often requires understanding the paradoxes of bringing them together in a way that generates new insight, new consciousness. I have the statement written there, but I want to pick up on a few of them. Our friend quotes Saint. Isaiah the Solitary saying that, "Without anger a man cannot attain purity. He has to feel anger for all that is sown in him by the enemy." So, right there we have the definition. The teachers of this ancient spiritual psychotherapy, this transformative spiritual discipline, is saying that human anger is not designed to be expelled upon others or a result of egotistical unmet desires or lack of self-control. This teacher, as others do, identifies the reality of anger as the inner weapon to struggle, to fight that spiritual warfare within – to give you the energy to encounter and face off with what he calls, "all that is sown in him by the enemy." And you could be more contemporary if you wish, even bringing Fourth Way teaching in that the step that goes on beyond self-observation is then combatting what one has observed to be the result of sleep and wrong work of the centers, of the emotions and so forth.

So understand that this is a whole new way of using what we call anger – utterly different. It's about inward towards that which is against our spiritual evolution. And he goes on to say, "He who wishes to acquire the anger that is in accordance with nature," by that he means for the purpose of spiritual development, "must uproot all self-will." Now that is paradoxical. We know anger as a self-will generated thing. It is our self-will that is the source of our anger much of the time. From earliest infancy, "No. I don't want to. You can't make me. You're not the boss of me." - all the way to our old age. And here he's speaking of a kind of energy, of force that only can exist if we uproot self-will. So, it is not about us even though it is for us, towards us that this force is directed. He goes on to say – the member asks about this use of anger in the Philokalia and how can it be reconciled with Buddha's teaching on practicing loving kindness towards a thought that has arisen?

Here you must realize that even though clearly we are speaking of universal truth, of openness to our teachings, there are specific traditions and paths that one must follow to accomplish one's aims. In other words, it cannot be just a smorgasbord of just a little bit of this and a little bit if that. Karlfried Graf Durkheim (whom so few know in the English speaking world) makes it clear to his students that one must choose a tradition and go all the way with that. Otherwise we end up with that sort of generic unrouted, undisciplined kind of thinking that leads nowhere. There has to be a determination and a focus and it so happens that in what we call Christianity, symbolized by the Cross, sacrifice is very much in the midst of it. That is to say crucifixion of the ego, self-denial in a sense that is not masochistic, but that is powerful and demanding, often brutal on oneself. The early teachers who were men and women of amazing compassion and mercy taught us to be merciless towards ourselves, not in some awful way, masochistic as I say, but to not allow the weakness, the luxury, the pandering to the ego that we pretty much live in all the time where number one is number one in the world and that's what's behind everything.

That elimination of the little self is key to the breakthrough – the breakdown of the walls that separate us from our deeper spiritual identity. So it is different from the way of the Buddha, which has all its wonderful deep intuitions, many of which can be tied into the teachings of Yeshua, but here we have a potent approach that is an all-or-nothing type of thing which has its special value especially in our time when we are so spoiled, so soft when it comes to dealing with ourselves. A student mentioned" "It seems to me that anger when consciously directed inward could be an effective tool," and fine words here, "to ignite action in pursuit of the aim. However the concern here is, the genuine concern, is that anger has manifested mostly negatively." There's no question and you can find in our books how negativity and anger is truly the enemy. The world lives on negativity, feeds on it. It is poison for ourselves, for our loved ones, the world – no question about it.

So this is a high point of discernment of telling the difference (*diakrisis* in Greek), a major technical, spiritual term for a methodology of the self-awareness, inward awareness that can see the difference between an anger that is destructive and negative and toxic and a holy anger, if you will, that has to do with here I stand against the bad habits, the hubris and vanity and all those other pathologies that we carry with us and that must be conquered by our own self-determination inspired by Spirit with the help of grace.

A student points out that that in fact, "Anger is responsible for bringing me from the low point from where I could begin to search with real purpose," very insightful perspective on themselves, maybe your own experience indeed. Anger can destroy our lives like alcohol or any other drug that we find ourselves, in fact, at rock bottom; we must start again. So understand that we are called to a quality of awareness and consciousness and self-mastery, self-remembering that brings with it a transcendence that is peace and compassion – that in fact the teaching is to take the suffering of life and transform it into steps towards higher consciousness and ancient Orthodoxy is one of the greatest psychological tools for how to do that – how to turn suffering into fuel for new being, for higher being, for a transcendence that takes us into what some call a sublime energy, chemically transforming the force of negativity into forgiveness and compassion.

And another question, "Is it even appropriate to attempt to equate anger and loving kindness as separate approaches to dealing with the adversary?" Very interesting. Is it appropriate to attempt to equate anger and loving kindnesses separate ways in dealing with the adversary and all that that implies? That is a profound question because in fact, it is out of loving kindness that such anger manifests towards that within which is inhibiting the indwelling of the -Holy Spirit – that is blocking the acquisition of the Holy Spirit - that is keeping us from being instruments precisely – incarnations of that loving kindness. So you can say that they are the same: two sides of a coin. And the key element I would say here is for you to reflect on an entirely different understanding of this "anger thing" that we can't get away from unless we figure out how to use it differently and that is part of the genius of the teachings of early Christianity.

It is part of the discernment of self-awareness that shows us the difference in those energies and ultimately the transformation of energies into higher consciousness from the crassness and darkness of anger to the transcendence of becoming – of purification, of overcoming oneself and becoming as some say, transparent to the Divine – a form of inner effort.

15

On the Friction of Life

All of us understand that life throws us curve balls and all sorts of other obstacles, some of them strangely intentional and metaphysical, others just accidents of life, but I want to honor our connection and your interest, which I hope is not one that fades easily when it comes to the deep things of life. I will be glad to give to you, always with the aim of bringing something practical and specific – wisdom for daily life rooted in the deepest wisdom.

Let us look at the subject of friction. We'll call it a technical word from Mr. Gurdjieff. We spoke of this before but it is important to be brought back to these cornerstone ideas. For the great Gurjieff, powerful master as you know, the very hardships of life, the very obstacles, the very horrors in the way of one's awakening, one's growth, were the fuel for the growth itself. I have tried to share that with the members of my church because this is the very essence or soul of the teaching of ancient Eastern Orthodoxy.

Most of you don't have the pleasure of *Branches*, a little holistic journal that here in Indianapolis has been alive and well for a number of years, but in it I have placed an article on these teachings on suffering.[2] But one of the references is to this man here, Saint Silouan the Athonite, one of the great saints of the early part of the twentieth century, a spiritual father to Father Sophrony who was another great teacher of our time and who was the spiritual mentor of my dear friends Father Alphonse and Rachel Goettmann, simply meaning there is magnificence in how we can all be connected.

And this image which we published or put in my article, happens to have a quote of Silouan which is, "*The man who cries out against evil men but does not pray for them will never know the Grace of God.*" Let that sink in because that is

---

[2] This article is available at http://innerworkforspiritualawakening.com/.

Holy Wisdom. Out of his deep suffering and humility and awakening to the presence of Christ consciousness he could say such a thing. And that is a pinnacle express one might say, of the Christian path although it's a universal oath which I'm sure you can all recognize, whether it comes from Buddhism or other places. But that special quality of grace and beauty of spirit present in that statement. Saint Silouan is also the one who said in his darkest hours, persecuted by fellow monks of course, that he received this vision, these words of the Christ saying *"Hold your soul in hell; do not despair."* And it carried him through and saved him and allowed him to become the great light that he was and continues to be long after his passing.

To hold your soul in hell and not despair is to manage to hang on to the faith in the reality of the spiritual realm, even in the harshest times of the physical realm, even when all seems lost and in fact if you want to climb the mountain of spiritual awakening, spiritual consciousness there must be that stage where we are taken to the far edge beyond what we can bear or think we can bear. And if we hang on in faith and trust, if we call upon the help of that spiritual reality, that miracle will happen and against all odds renewal, new beginnings, redemption, can take place. This is a verifiable, magnificent experience that I know personally, that I know others have experienced, and that you can experience. So, from the point of view of the Fourth Way all the difficulties of life become firewood for the fire. In other words, strengthen your consciousness, raise your consciousness to another level of perspective and transcendence so that you can walk calmly through the nightmare and holding on through that dark night you will achieve a new level of faith, understanding, and relationship with the spiritual reality.

If some of you are in times of great suffering and all of us walk that path somehow sometime, remember that and take it seriously for it is one of the pearls of great price and discover that the very negative things of life, personal and destructive can turn into the fertilizer for your soul, the awakening of a deeper self, and the face-to-face encounter with the reality of God's help.

16

Buffers and Personality

We have an especially interesting question here for all of you who are seeking to work on yourselves to apply these teachings. This one of the kinds of questions that I really enjoy receiving because it is specific and multi-layered and deeply engaged with work ideas. The question relates to buffers and I'll remind you that The Work, the Fourth Way uses buffers as a technical term to describe the psychological phenomena that allows us to unconsciously compartmentalize all the different parts of ourselves so that one part doesn't know the other part – that we think we're nice, gentle people and forget when we are violently enraged, and we think we are spiritual people but have lust and envy and all kinds of other things going on. So there's no way to unify this fragmentation, this multiplicity and the teaching tells us that there exists this amazing set of blinders that allows us to think we are one person for a period of time and live in that illusion even while being another person. Surely all of you can see that in some way. It's the Dr. Jekyll – Mr. Hyde thing multiplied a thousand times.

The person asks, "Is it necessary for one to see these buffers in one's own life, or is it even possible to see them?" Now that's getting intricate. Can you see that which compartmentalizes you – that which hides from you, that other part of yourself for the moment. Is it even possible to see that? The person goes on to say, "Is it even necessary to see how the buffers are working against me? Or is it enough to just focus my attention observing the false I's?"

This takes us to the heart of the practical work here. We know that this idea of buffers exists, which explains why we think we're great even though people around us can see different. People that we are in relationship with know us better than we know ourselves. We live in that unreality of who we think we are, fueled by features and vanity and all that. So how does one see this? And I would say that it is true that what you can actually perceive – catch in the moment of attention – when you have divided your attention and you are seeing within as well as without, not captivated just by the out and being a stimulus-response mechanism that just unconsciously responds - seeing shall we say, that violent "I," knowing it to be not merely false but toxic, ungodly – the opposite of who we are born to be – the enemy, darkness – whatever you want to bring to it from all traditions and teachings that identify us. Seeing the contradiction between that person that we are in that moment and the person that we are in another moment is the way we discover our state of affairs, our multiplicity.

The buffer in between is not a thing to see though. You are correct in that. Just the power of that inner blindness which is illuminated by the strength of that observing eye. The more you are able to objectively observe – do not identify with it (meaning get caught up in it, feel guilty and judgment and all of that). See it for what it is;

have the honesty to do that, which is very rare for all of us. This is hard work. This is the true spiritual discipline. To recognize that you are this person in one moment and this totally different person in this other moment is enough to allow you to recognize that multiplicity and know that the aim is to pull out of that multiplicity, that legion, that fragmentation in order to rise to that real "I," that more unified essence, that essential person that is within, that is connected to Spirit and is not the chaotic mess which we are.

We can see that humanity is a chaotic mess and that is an external manifestation of the internal level of being or condition of each person. So, it is not necessary to see how the buffers are working and that is an important and very clear perception on the member's part – that it is enough to focus on all these different "I"s and recognize them as false, as not you.

The student goes on to say, "I don't seem to notice them [these buffers] in my own personality," –and that is because what there is to notice is multiplicity. So, in a sense you are going too clinical trying to find the fabric that might separate these strange, different people in you. "Is this something that I will observe with continued work? Or are buffers something just to be aware of in terms of "the big picture" with regard to realizing how they can keep one's acquired personality from seeing all of the false "I"s?" That is the correct conclusion that allows us to know that there is a mechanical way, even an organic way that keeps us in that lower state of consciousness and so understanding the idea of buffers simply allows us to recognize that indeed we absolutely compartmentalize all the different pieces of ourselves so that one does not know the other and live in imagination that we are one.

So that is the key and the assistance of knowing an idea like a buffer simply allows us to see the panorama and understand why it is that way – why in the world, as Paul says – Saint Paul - "Why do I do the things I don't want to do?" The very question that's at the heart of this psychological, spiritual work. So, once again, it is about inner self-observation, growing in objectivity and strength in creating an inner space within that is not whatever is manifesting so that even if you are in an "I" that is angry and cannot get out of it, yet there is something within some element of attention that allows you to know that this is not who you really are. This is not who you want to be and as time goes on and you put more force into that observing "I" and pull force out of the false "I"s that are not you, then you begin to weaken this state of affairs and the buffers are no longer able to keep you unaware of your reality of what needs to be worked on. So that question just brings us back to the core practices, inner separation, divided attention, self-observation. These fabulous spiritual truths, unknown to mainstream spirituality and yet rooted in the deepest of wisdom – they work, they will change you if you have the honesty and courage and devotion to the great aim of becoming transparent to the Divine – becoming connected to your spirit – becoming who you are, who you were before life beat you up and turned you into what you were not. So let it be a great reminder for all of us to do this work today, right now in these moments of our lives.

17

Observing I

How does the Observing "I" notice our condition, our human condition without judgment and without condemning? Observing "I" ought to be a liberating thing to separate. That's why we start Fourth Way teachings with Divided Attention. To separate yourself from what you're looking at in itself is liberation. You are not that, you are not the polluted thoughts, you are not the sinful thoughts. You know sin in its original meaning is not a bunch of different things, a laundry list. I'm sure you've heard this is my sermons, *hamartano* or missing the mark – like the archer missing the bull's eye. It's missing the mark of life, so Observing "I" is not about seeing all the bad things we do, it's about discovering our true identity is not being that. Our true identity is in a place of tranquility and in that tranquility we are able to – it's like seeing from a high mountain or a high building – we witness our human condition which is just like our brothers and sisters. We recognize what doesn't work, what isn't the right way to go and we let go and we forgive and we are not that. You are not that. Think of what liberation that is. You are not that negative thought. So Observing "I" is the beginning of freedom, inner separation that allows you not only to stop certain things, to make choices, but to recognize that your identity is not in the lower part of yourself, not in the crowd of "I"s themselves that are all fragmented and messy and full of worry and anger and so forth.

We are creating the beginnings of crossing the threshold of a self that is beautiful, free, so it's very different from the old style religion, the ignorant religion that is unrelated to the original religion – the original religion coming from the Apostolic age with Jesus and His disciples was about theosis, deification, the image of God coming alive in us. God became man so that man may become god. That's spooky and yet marvelous! The

Spirit entered humanity, our humanity so that humanity could be lifted up into spiritual consciousness, to speak in modern terms. So whatever you see about yourself is not seeing you, because that which is seeing is you. You see what I mean? You are much more than what you are seeing and so you mustn't judge it – that's what we keep saying all the time. You must recognize that it is the beginning of new self. The old person, the old man and the new man – new creature in Christ, as Paul says.

So that all that is not appropriate or wrong work or bad habits or things we picked up from life or wars of life are no longer who we are. Observing "I" leads us into that spiritual place that is not wounded, but linked directly with purity of heart, Spirit. So whatever pollution you see, don't identify with it - which means don't take it as yourself. Make a space with it so that your self, your real self is not that. And then you begin to have empowerment to become that child of God who is not the sum total of the mess of life.

18

The Mastery of Thoughts

This addresses a two part question. The first one has to do with applying these teachings on self-awareness, self-observation that come out of both early Christianity, Fourth Way, and other authentic spiritual traditions. Once one has witnessed the wrong work within oneself, the misperceptions, the negative attitude, the personality flaws, the ways of thinking and seeing that come to us from imitation of parents and others - once we begin to see that, then what is the next step? What do we do about it and that is a very valuable question. How do we then transform all that and become freed from it?

That is indeed the transformational process, the *metanoia* as it says in the Biblical Greek, the turning around – the formation of the deeper self where these are not present. To observe something in yourself that you know is wrong – a wrong work we'll call it – is not good for your own spiritual cleanliness and advancement – requires indeed the beginning of a spiritual battle. One in which the decision is made upon seeing that, to not allow it to have power. To not allow oneself to fall into the familiar patterns and momentum that cause it to exhibit itself and to become center state in your life so that the observation of this problem area, by the mere fact that it is seen from a more objective point of view allows one to recognize that it is not oneself that one is looking at.

We are not that; we are that deeper self, that consciousness that is able to witness this and therefore we are also able to generate the willpower to choose not to continue along those lines, not to just go with the flow, but indeed to go against the current – sort of like the salmon going upstream against the flow of the water, back to its source to fulfill its true purpose.

There comes a time in these inner efforts where one is sensitized to such an extent that the negativity of the wrong work, of the judgmentalism, of the jealousy, fear – whatever it might be – the rage – with that energy comes a very bad taste. You become much more aware of how poisoness and damaging it is to ourselves, not to speak of to others. And the choice becomes easier to make – to not go with that – to take that energy and transmute it. This is part of that alchemical process of old to turn that energy into something else such as intensified presence where the energy rises up into just being present rather than losing it all and letting it all flow out of one through that wrong function. In that effort you find that we desperately need all of that wasted life force in order to create that quality of higher consciousness.

It takes energy for that and we are constantly leaking out that energy in wrong ways – "leaking cisterns that can hold no water," says the prophet Jeremiah. So to observe that which is not right then requires of us that we begin to not act on it. Then we begin to move the power of false personality, then we begin to claim that moment – that life force for something greater and nobler and we discover in fact, that we can do that. And in doing that we expand the strength of that which is observing, we enable peace of mind and heart, deeper sight, deeper compassion and empathy, all of these elements that require the fuel that is so wasted in how we live our lives. So having seen that which is not functioning right, one must begin to dismantle into, in fact go against the current and function right and recognize that we have been sort of captivated. Overtaken by personality, how to function in the world – much of it artificial but useful and necessary and let it run our lives at the cost, at the expense of our essential self, of our essence. And it is that return to essence that becomes a great yearning in our lives.

We no longer need to be that construct that we have created consciously and unconsciously – mostly unconsciously. And soon, that essential self begins to be the more present, active part of our being and all that is egocentric and twisted about our personality begins to fade into the background.

So dare to take that baby step, that first step, that plunge into not being the way you have been before for the sake of a higher purpose – for the sake of your higher self and discover for yourself what difference it will make. God bless you on this journey of awakening, of spiritual evolution, of greater purpose and consciousness in this world.

19

Chief Feature and the Connection to Body Types

The following question is part of the effort to understand how we function according to the profound insights of the Fourth Way which provide a language which, like a compass, helps us come to know ourselves.

The question before us is: "Will a person's Chief Feature always be in some way connected to the Chief Features as listed in the material on body types? Or can they be something completely different?" The classic Chief Feature is the axis around which everything comes out of us – all of our stimulus response, all of our motivation, the hidden key to how we function automatically through our make-up. We are born with this foundational motivating factor embedded in our being.

For instance, the Lunar type who stays up late at night, who's a little odd, who's got a small chin, who's a little different and highly introspective typically has the Chief Feature of willfulness because that is the power which his mechanism has available to him. We know that the Venusian type, so full of nurturing and gentleness is often "non-existent," meaning that you hardly notice them because they are so passive, and there is nothing wrong with that. It is what it is.

We know that the Mercurial type tends to have power as their Chief Feature. They tend to be the flashy type, high energy and the "life of the party." Many actors are Mercurial. Their kind of power feature, which is very different than the Martial type, is much more manipulative, tricky and often includes lying. This is not a judgment, but an objective fact that you can observe for yourself if you study these matters.

The Saturn type – tall and long-boned, slow to speak – tends to exhibit a feature of dominance. This type doesn't need to say a word and yet is in control of those around him or her. The Martial type is the warrior and typically ruled by a power feature of course. This type is often a bull in a china shop – telling it like it is, stepping on people's toes, fighting for justice. Then on the Enneagram of Essence types comes the Jovial who is surrounded by people, is a great host, and has a brilliant mind quite often and generally motivated by the feature of vanity because they know how wonderful they are. They tend to suffer from periodicity – it's really hard to finish a project, just like Orson Welles who would get tired of or bored with making a movie in the middle of making it.

This is a very basic summary of behaviors that you can observe as you study the types. To answer the above question, people can be of a certain type and have something else that is their primary engine block or motivating factor. It might be fear, for instance. The Martial type, with his adrenalin (or her adrenalin) pumping tall the time, could be functioning from a chief feature of fear because adrenalin causes fight or flight. The Lunar could be so filled with vanity that he's a megalomaniac and many of them strangely are even though they are often anti-social and in many ways rejected by social groups due to their tendency to be a little different.

It can be the case that there is are individual differences in the dynamics that drive us automatically. One thing is certain: All the types have vanity as an important component. It is sadly unavoidable, but on the other hand it gives us something with which to work, something with which to face off, to overcome, to observe, to recognize, to see how it is an obstacle to breaking through and letting a higher nature come through.

We will always be working out of our mechanics, but the development of conscious awareness, of liberation from our stimulus-response reactions that often damage our life, that make us go around in circles forever repeating the same things, can be used for good. The Martial type with deeper wisdom and a detachment from the fire of adrenalin can be a marvelous, loyal companion. The Lunar can be a brilliant scientist even in his or her isolation, introspection, and oddity. They can help save the world with their focus on their particular interest.

So do not look at these teachings as judgment or condemnation. Accept them. That requires humility which necessary to do this inner work, and which is why so few will do it. They do not want to face themselves — to see themselves truly. Sometimes it is helpful to have a spouse point things out and to accept the "photograph" as it is called. Such acceptance helps us understand ourselves better.

But let there be no question that we need not remain what we have always been and we *can* incarnate through the type that we are -- through the features we have -- something of a higher order, something spiritual and unified around the love of God, around goodness, and devotion to something higher than ourselves. That changes everything because then we enter into the realm of the True Self which is not captive to these varieties of unconscious, mechanical ways. Keep observing; see it in others and you will learn so much.

PART THREE

Two roads diverged in a wood, and I
I took the one less traveled by,
And that has made all the difference.
Robert Burns

20

On Faith and Forgiveness

The following question deals with the connection, integration, link between the Fourth Way teachings and all that comes along with that and the deep, fundamental spiritual revelation, teachings of Christianity. For instance, the concept of forgiveness – and not merely forgiveness, but forgiveness of sins as in God forgives me of my sins and I have faith that he does that.

How does that fit into what is presented here? How does it fit in with self-observation? How does it fit in with the mechanics, if you will, of the Gnosis teaching that is shared in this particular manner and vocabulary through the Fourth Way, which essentially parallels also the teachings of early Christianity as I pointed out many times. So, the seeming paradox of work on oneself and the impact of the knowledge of ultimate, unconditional love and forgiveness - Grace of God, as well as faith and prayer as the life giving experience of relationship with Spirit ties into the work process in that we are laying the groundwork to participate in that or to anticipate or to become receptive to that very gift and knowing of the Holy One's presence, of our dependence on that which is greater than we are.

This higher consciousness journey is to become more conscious of the real and the real, spiritually speaking, is encountered by those who know how to encounter or are gifted with encountering the light – encountered as forgiveness and if one truly felt in the depths of one's being the impact of loving forgiveness as a living reality, as a healing touch from the Living One, from the Mystery that has created us and yet is intimately present to us – that was the very purpose of Christ's mission – creating that intimate, experiential communion with the Holy as mortal beings – eternity present in time, so self-remembering and all those tools of attention – use of attention, awareness of self, change of behavior, objective observation on that is precisely to open the door for this next phase of development of spiritual awakening. It is true that it was not discussed in the books that you'll find typically, certainly not by Ouspensky, although it was Ouspensky in his final meetings who spoke of Mount Athos and students go there to find tradition as some of you know is classic book his classic book *In Search of the Miraculous*, he originally titled *Fragments of an Unknown Teaching*. What was unknown and what that teaching was (unknown to Ouspensky) turns out to be the early Eastern, Christian Gnosis, knowledge, teaching, revelation that exploded into the world and came out of those areas: Syria and so forth as a radical transformation of a human being into a greater resemblance of God. Be children of light is what they were called, so the link, the connection is there, but you discover it in your experience.

Don't wait for somebody to write a book on it; don't expect the old books to talk about it because Gurjieff knew that the people of – the intellectual Europeans of the 1920s and 30s were not interested in hearing about Christianity. They had turned their backs on it and they knew nothing of Eastern Orthodox spirituality which was the birthplace, the mentoring, and the development of Gurdjieff, even with his other studies in Sufi connections and so forth. So to summarize, all of that which you feel is essential to your sense of what you find in the teachings of Christ, is to be found through the methodologies of the Fourth Way whether it is directly mentioned or not. It is the opening, the beginning first steps of the journey. Thank you for this question. I hope you can practice it and discover it for yourself.

21

The Mystery of the Sign of the Cross

The following material is a rare and profound expression of the meaning of the Sign of the Cross, revealing that it is more than ritual, but rather a profound expression of that which is holy, that which is of ancient times and filled with wisdom and meaning for each of us. These are the words of Pierre Erny, a professor Emeritus of Anthropology at Strasbourg and author of numerous books, originally published in *Le Chemin (The Path)*, a quarterly journal filled with the profound teachings of Eastern Christian spirituality and presented by Father Alphonse and Rachel Goettmann. They are co-founders of Bethanie, a Center of Spiritual Encounter in eastern France and an Orthodox community.

We are told the Sign of the Cross is one of the most ancient and universal gestures that can be found in our time. It goes back to the Apostolic era – the era of the first Apostles. But if we are relatively knowledgeable regarding our ancestors in the faith – texts and writing of every kind – we often miss descriptions of the way in which they expressed their various liturgical and pious gestures which they did in private moments.

This gesture is one of those things which can only be experienced and is difficult to write about, therefore we are uncertain as to the way in which the sign of the cross was practiced throughout Christian history – the mutations it went through, and the various ways in which the faithful came to use it. But the point here is not to proceed from the ritual but to show that it is overflowing with a wealth of wisdom, a wealth we can draw from deeply and which belonged to the Christians of yesteryear – the state of consciousness in which they lived daily, an initiation into their own experience which is transmitted through the Tradition.

It is difficult to invent a liturgical gesture, and many have tried different ways. But before we invent something, would it not be a good idea to give life to that which existed from the beginning and proved itself so valuable? You might be surprised to find that, in the humble Sign of the Cross, there is a veritable recapitulation of the Christian Faith – a way to make present in the soul and in the body the great Truths that structured the life of the believer. The Trinity, the Incarnation, salvation, right relations between the human and the Divine - all of this is part of the Sign of the Cross.

Here we will talk about the gesture – its physical manifestation. In this simple act are included the theology of the Cross received according to the spirituality of the Apostolic times, and the teachings of the Holy Fathers on the Trinity and on redemption.

In studying this gesture, we are struck by the profound unity of inspiration which characterizes its practice in the midst of Christian life as well as the diversity of the way it is done according to the cultures and epochs, wherever the Church was found. We will look at the gesture itself, the direction, the parts of the body involved, and where it is done, as well as the positions of the fingers and the words that come with it.

Let us look at ancient Christianity. It tells us that the Sign of the Cross begins at the forehead, with the thumb and the first two fingers of the right hand placed together. Tertullian, born in Africa around the year 200, states: "At every step, in every movement, in entering and leaving, in putting on our clothing and our shoes, in lighting our lamps, in going to bed and sitting down – in all our occupations, let us mark our forehead with the sign of the Cross."

In his treatise, he speaks to his beloved wife. This gesture is therefore present in the most intimate settings. It also has a liturgical function in which he brings the Catechumen – the learner – into the very rite of Baptism and the transformation of our human ways. This little sign which we impress upon ourselves is found as well in the crosses traced during the greeting among the early Christians, sharing the peace of the Holy.

How have we gone from this gesture expressed in the simplest way to its more meaningless usage today? It was discreet, known only to the faithful in order to recognize each other without awakening the attention of the godless. It served as a way of creating an environment within the material world which connected with Eternity.

Whenever we make the sign of the cross, it moves from above to below. The reasons given are the following: The Son is engendered by the Father who is greater than He is. The Son descends from heaven to earth for the salvation of the world; he takes flesh in the heart of the virgin.

The vertical movement from above to below marks the eruption of the Divine into history and into the human condition, linking the Creator with His creatures. But it can also take a more anthropological meaning: it is formed at the head, the level of ideas, and only becomes fertile when it descends into the level of the heart. Then it is integrated, no longer merely external, by the whole person.

Intelligence is cold; what it produces must be warmed. The movement from the forehead to the chest indicates the necessity to bring everything into one's interior center, one's depths -- there where the Kingdom of God is already present, where is expressed the human in the Divine.

22

Symbolism and the Sign of the Cross

First and foremost, we must place the gesture in the context of the practices which come out of the life of the Church, and the habits taken up again and again in the worship experience.

Different cases can obviously be presented for the power and value of this ritual, but it is not typical that in this second case we try to add to these practices or onto these practices meanings that are more or less pertinent, that is they may not be the point of these ancient teachings. They can present great interest at the level of learning, of understanding the historical context and the catechism associated with it since they give meaning to things and allow to concretely illustrate the great truths of the Faith by inscribing them literally on our body.

This is what is of interest to us. Let us take several examples that do not seek to completely express all that can be said about this domain of the Holy manifesting through matter – Spirit through matter -- but at least let us try to get a taste of that which enables new discoveries for each person who intentionally and consciously applies these ancient ways.

We begin with that vertical movement from above to below. The tracing of the Sign of the Cross from above to below is done because the Son is engendered by the Father who is greater and the Son who descends from above – from beyond upon the earth for the salvation of humanity.

So the vertical movement from above to below therefore expresses the eruption of the Divine into history – into your history, *into your moment* each time you do this. The Divine enters into our very condition, linking the Creator with the creature – the Uncreated One with the created. When you make the sign with intention you are linking yourself with the ineffable as it enters into your reality. That which forms within our mind from the realm of ideas only becomes fertile when it descends in to the heart. So we take knowledge into the heart – integrating all of this into our personhood. The movement from the forehead to the chest therefore indicates the necessity to *bring everything into the interior center of our being,* there where life germinates, where the Kingdom of God is already present, where is expressed the human and the Divine. Let these words of wisdom seep into your understanding, because if you can manifest this in such a simple act, what power comes through!

We find in the writings of the Great Saint Maximus the Confessor (seventh century) an idea no doubt taken from the stoics, stating that it is good for the intelligence, which is cold, to be warmed by the heart since the heart is in fact warm by its very nature. So this vertical movement of the hand in the Sign of the Cross reminds us of this mystical event. That which is produced in the head must be warmed in the heart to become fruitful. There are three types of intimate constitutions of the person which oppose such a process:

First, there are those whose intelligence and whose hearts are already warm. These are the idealists, full of zeal, often confused, but inefficient.

Second, there are those whose intelligence (intellect) and whose heart are cold. They know how to analyze with finesse. They are careful, detailed, but they are indifferent and frozen towards others.

Third, there are those whose intelligence is warm but whose heart is cold. These are the ideologues who know how to seduce others by their ideas, but will not back away from any cruelty when it comes to putting them into practice.

In the tracing of the cross three times before the reading of Holy Scripture -- forehead, chest, mouth -- we evoke the Word of God which must fall within the earth of our body and of our heart in order to germinate. It it is like opening our being to inspiration of holy teaching. In the West, we have often been satisfied by images that tend toward the naturalist way of thinking and so the catechism of the Portuguese at the end of the sixteenth century would teach to a child that he or she must carry the hand way below the chest because through His incarnation, Jesus descended deep into the being of the virgin Mary – yet another wonderful symbol.

Then we have the horizontal movement, either from right to left or from left to right. You may know the Orthodox are from right to left, the Catholics are left to right. Why does this matter? If the verticality of the symbol or movement indicates the depth of the Sign of the Cross, the horizontality signifies extension, deployment, expansion, propagation, dilation, development, action of the will, and openness to others. It is therefore normal to be *linked with the Holy Spirit* which fills the whole universe.

After the first commandment, "You will love the Lord your God," comes the second, "and you will love your neighbor as yourself." To speak and to act before having matured in one's heart, through an impulse coming from above, leads to a sterile activism no matter how good our intentions. Therefore, the horizontal movement corresponds to the gesture of the creating God separating the waters from above from the waters below, having separated light from darkness vertically.

23

Transformation and the Sign of the Cross

According to the ancient Tradition, we find here one of the major keys of the Christian rite. Saint Augustine tells us that the right side belongs to all that comes from eternal life, that reveals eternal life, whereas the left belongs to that which is from temporal existence. going from right (eternity) to left (our brief journey, our mortal life). No one has ever even had the thought to assume that the sign of the cross should be traced with the left hand due to the primeval understanding of right and left. When a rite must be accomplished with only one hand, such as benediction, a chrismation, an unction, the presentation of offerings, or the distribution of communion, it is necessarily done with the right hand.

When both sides of the body must be taken into account, we always begin with the right. According to Cyril of Jerusalem, the believer received the Body of Christ in his right hand, with the left hand forming a foundation which is holding up the right hand. That is indeed how we hold our hands when we receive the blessing from the priest, as well as the bread.

When the celebrant must turn towards himself, he does it from the right side. He does this as well when he turns around an object such as the altar for incensing it. In the way, prayer was done in the direction of the East where the liturgical elements and edifices were present. The south – warm and luminous -- is identified with the East and the right. Whereas the north -- cold and dark – is identified with the left. In the traditional ordinance of the Church, microcosm of humanity, we find the expression of the macrocosm and its dimensions expressed through our bodies. These simple points allow us to understand the importance that is placed upon our going from the right to the left in this symbolic manner: From eternity to the temporal, from the Divine to the human.

A current interpretation in Orthodox circles suggests following: The right side symbolizes righteousness, the left side compassion. The second one must always follow the first one. It is out of becoming righteous, or aligned with the Holy, that compassion comes forth. Another interpretation suggests that the movement from right to left imitates the enlightenment at the end of time which goes from the East to the West.

The movement from left to right has also been explained as representing the passage from death to life, from darkness to life, from hell to paradise, from sin to innocence, from perdition to salvation. Pope Innocent the Third said: "Some do the Sign of the Cross from left to right because we must pass from misery to glory just as Christ passed from death to life and from His journey from darkness to paradise."

Psychologists have shown intuitively how our civilization goes from left to right, in the direction of the sun. The very arrows of our watches, as well as Latin writing move from left to right. Therefore, this movement follows the greater movement of history and progress, from within to without, from the past to the future.

On the other hand, to go from right to left is a more regressive, introverted way. It is to swim against the current, to go back to the past, to the origins, to the mother, to go from the exterior to the interior, from reality to its principle, from effect to cause. Seen in this way, the Latin gesture and the Greek gesture both offer an entirely different tonality.

This movement brings us into alignment with a certain tonality as we make the Sign of the Cross.

Regarding the position of the fingers: The first finger represents the origin and the foundation of all that is Divine, that which is at the heart of all things since all other numbers are formed according to it. The second finger invokes the encounter – the couple, distinction, opposition, war, conjunction, separation, dialogue and clash, instability, but also the power of evolution, the call to mediation of a third, a synthesis. So the three fingers represent the surmounting of opposition, the fruitful encounter, the stability of being.

The fourth finger is the image of balance and accomplishment and the fifth represents the entire hand, plentitude, the being of each person as fruit of a becoming that is centered – mastered and harmonious. The teachings of the ancient Church tell us that the firs three fingers represent the Trinity, and the last two fingers represent natures of Christ -- human and Divine.

Finally, this teaching speaks of the symbolic importance of the different parts of the body. The body is structured around the spinal cord and the bones that cross the shoulders carry the Cross inscribed in the most intimate part of our being. The forehead, the face, the senses, the shoulders represent the horizontality which is open to the world and the others.

The chest, the stomach, the arms and the hands, are all symbolic of how we exist in the world. Let us look at just a few. The forehead represents the most elevated part of the body – the one which is considered the most noble, the one from which come the commandments which are registered in the rest of the organism. In sanctifying the forehead by the cross, we hope to touch our being in its entirety. The face represents, along with the hand, that part of our organism which is deeply personal, that which, through sight and hearing, taste and smell, is most apt to capture all that comes to us from the world.

The chest, where is concentrated the functions of air and blood, is the location of these changes operated within the body through the circulation that comes from without, such as breathing in, and the outward return through expiration. The heart is not only the seat of feeling and emotion, but also the symbol of the human being who is conscious in the most profound dimension of his or her interior being.

Going from the fact that shame is read so easily on the human face, Saint Augustine tells us that that the tracing of the Cross on the forehead and across the face means that we glorify the entire victory of Christ's work on us without shame. The saint's commentary in the Canticle of Canticles tells us that Christ is the seal that is posed on the forehead, the heart, and the arms so that we are always enabled to love. This seal on the arm reminds us that we can act rightly; the seal on that render our face luminous in our loving, luminous in our acts of mercy so that Christ's entire being takes form within us.

That is the meaning and spiritual power of this simple and all-powerful act – the center of Christian worship according to the ancient and original ways. May you discover it for yourself.

24

Controlling the Mind

You need to master your thoughts; you need to be able to separate them so the thoughts that talk about the dishwasher have got to take a back seat to the thought that is all about "I want unity with God." That's going to be the smallest thing, the smallest part of it and we've got to build it up. We've got to gather, unify around that so there's strength and power and will and determination. Otherwise you're just going to be a never-ending chaotic mess. My dear friends the Goettmans say, Once you make that one decision, that unique decision, then you are on the way if you hold on to it, but we have to commit to that decision: I'm going to walk that spiritual journey, make it my life even if there's a million other things I have to do, because then you know it's important and begin to truly see. If you don't have an aim, it's random chaos and you never get anywhere.

So, that guiding principle helps you discern, "Okay, forget about the laundry right now. Focus on what is truly important." That's why suffering is a great teacher because suffering puts things in order. It makes it clear what's important. You all know what I'm talking about. I know that you have no doubt lived that human suffering from whatever you've been through and in suffering it becomes all that is important. And we have to give that dimension of energy and significance to how we live our daily life. And the simplicity – the simplest thing of our thoughts is what gets in the way, which is why we have to have a focused will to know the intention, to know what we are doing and why, to know what's important and when. And only you can determine that in your life.

You have all the freedom in the world. You're not in a monastery; the Abbot is not telling you what to do. You're not dealing with vows of obedience. You are responsible for determining what's important. If nothing has priority, then anything goes and that's part of being mechanical, being a body type. If you're a passive Venusian, it's more difficult to have a powerful presence as opposed to the warrior type. But you've got willpower and you've got yearning in your heart and the great teachers say, "You must make that choice, that decision," that becomes the compass of your life. And then everything takes its rightful place.

If you look at the great saints, Saint Francis and so many saints, they were people of amazing willpower – one thought, one purpose and that's a unification of their being. It's the unification of the fragmentation that's around that one thing and that's what gives us new strength, new motivation to come out of our chaos and of our confusion and it doesn't have to be a traumatic battle.

The Goettmanns speak of "effortless effort." It isn't tension; it isn't stress. It isn't that kind of strained effort, but it is a decision – a determination – a reminder that we have – that death is not distant from any of us. We have limited time and therefore we must use it rightly, especially when we are privileged to be given this kind of knowledge. And what you're looking for needs to now penetrate into the marrow of your bones. Not getting a bunch more information, not fascination with the esoteric and the mysterious there's plenty of that, but to be able to begin to do one thing and to protect it.

You set boundaries from within, first of all. Boundaries where certain parts of yourself aren't going to rule, aren't going to run the show, but rather be servants to that part of you that recognizes your true purpose in life. That part of you is what you must keep strengthened whether it's beginning with that meditative thing on a regular basis, not allowing thoughts to constantly fill your mind – you know. Discover your weak points and then deal with them.

You know there is a harsh metaphor from the Holy Father, you've heard me say it no doubt, "When the snake skips in from under the door, cut off its head." What does that mean? When some thought that is not related to your aim of higher consciousness in relation to God, comes in and wants to take over, be merciless with it. Take the action you must take so that you can protect the sacredness of your inner space. That's the glory of the Fourth Way. It is all available to us who live in the world. You don't have to be cloistered; you don't have to get up at three in the morning to pray or sing. You can live life as it is in a world that is totally secular, as you know and keep that inner sanctuary alive, where your individuality, your individualization, as Jung says, remains intact and you are able to accomplish that which you seek to accomplish even if nobody else does.

25

The Experience of Grace

Grace is one of the most powerful, profound words in spirituality. It is one of those terms which seeks to reference that which cannot be put into words, that which can only be experienced. There is no doubt that many of us have had experiences of Grace in our lives and perhaps have not realized what was happening to us. The experience of Grace is the immediate encounter with the reality of Divine Presence, its active role in our daily lives, incarnated in what seems like the most ordinary events – the right book at the right time, meeting a particular person, changes in life circumstances that lead to a whole new chapter in one's spiritual maturing.

Those encounters are characterized by moments when a great peace overtakes us, or a state of inexplicable gratitude and joy, even in the midst of pain and uncertainty. The ancient ones of Eastern Christianity speak of "Grace-filled people," individuals who carry a light within that radiates out as an unconditional love which is so rare that it is not of this world. And yet, it is at the heart of Creation. Grace is the infinite power of the Goodness of the Living One making itself known, making the impossible possible -- from forgiving the unforgivable to the redemption of a life and the creation of the new person we thought we could never be. The tide of circumstances can be dramatically turned, making something beautiful out of great hardship.

You might say that Grace is the energy, the living current of God running through the material world and made known to receptive hearts. Many people have had these "starry moments" as one philosopher calls them, where life is experienced so vividly that one feels connected and therefore "at one" with all things of life. This is a quality of consciousness that is Grace-given and though we must do the groundwork to help increase the potential for these wondrous experiences in our lives, it is always mixed with that unexpected gift from another dimension.

Since Grace is the power of the Holy One, it has many purposes. Sometimes it is Grace for someone to fail or to make a mistake, guiding them in another direction so that out of the negative event comes something life-changing that we could not have conceived on our own. Only Grace can give us the self-transcendent ability to love our enemies and this tells us that the goal of life, the direction the spiritual journey, is to live moment to moment in that state of Grace which can be understood as awareness of the Holy, receptivity to its guidance and direction, as well as gratefulness for its protection. In this spiritually polluted world of ours where psychosis and dark behavior are common, the light of Grace is needed more than ever in human life. Left to ourselves, we can only degenerate as is being witnessed all around us.

Grace is also the burning fire of conscience urging us to right action or to remorse for wrong action. One of the factors in human life that generates this transcendent experience of bliss and gratitude is often fueled by suffering. All of us suffer in this life in varying degrees, some more intensely than others, but we all know that life is not a "rose garden" and no one escapes its difficulties – emotionally and physically. Sometimes it is when those most traumatic of experiences take place that we have the opportunity to be flooded by that which is called Grace. When the heart is broken, when you are deeply betrayed, when people speak falsely against you, try to find the inner strength not to crack under the injustice and maliciousness of others. Choose not to be filled with rage or despair. Then you are "letting go" or detaching yourself from this most intimate kind of pain, and a door will open. As the great spiritual teacher Karlfried Graf Durckheim said: *"Open the door and let yourself be found."*

In these first steps of self-transcendence, looking past our own trauma, we become attuned and receptive to another power. The ancient teachers of early eastern Christianity masterfully taught how to turn suffering into regeneration rather than destruction. In a little handwritten note, hidden away and discovered many years after his death, Father Seraphim Rose crystallized into a few words the essence of a great truth for our times: "*Pain of heart* is the *condition* for spiritual growth and the manifestation of God's power. Healings occur to those in desperation, in hearts pained but still trusting and hoping in God's help. This is when God acts."

Why do people learn through pain and suffering, and not through pleasure and happiness? Very simply, because pleasure and happiness accustom one to satisfaction with the things given in this world, whereas pain and suffering drive one to seek a more profound happiness beyond the limitations of this world. But in pleasure we are content with what we have. In the Patristic writings, "*pain of heart*" generally refers to an elemental inward suffering, the bearing of an interior cross, and a spirit broken in contrition.

If used in the right way, suffering can purify the heart, and *the pure in heart shall see God* (Matt. 5:8). "The right approach," wrote Father Seraphim Rose, "is found in the heart which tries to humble itself and simply knows that it is suffering, and that there somehow exists a higher truth which can not only help this suffering, but can bring it into a totally different dimension." One of the deepest sayings I have found in my studies comes from Mark the Ascetic in the sixth century: *"Pain of heart is remembrance of God endured in a spirit of devotion."* This is one of those teachings that must be quietly absorbed and contemplated in order to be understood. Another mighty spiritual guide of that Tradition who lived in the early twentieth century, Saint Silouan, a monk of Mount Athos, during his time of deepest darkness had a vision of the Christ who told him: *"Hold your soul in hell and do not despair."* Those words enabled him to hang on through the suffering until that time when an inner light filled him and liberated him from his agony, turning him into one of the most luminous saints of the modern age.

So Grace is not some supernatural thing that we can only hope for, but rather it is an interaction with the spiritual dimension of life, and though we cannot make it happen, we must certainly believe that it can. Saint Augustine, leading Teacher of the western church for a thousand years, stated that "God is closer to us than our own breath," and, indeed, when we accept to be dependent on a higher power and allow ourselves to be helped by this forgotten Presence, we participate through our free will in the manifestation of that great mystery of Goodness called Grace which can utterly transform our lives, from darkness to light, from despair to joy. It is the "pearl of great price" to remain open to such a possibility in all the moments of our existence.

26

Taking the Narrow Path

That "road less traveled by" is a modern parallel to the ancient mystical metaphor *"the way is narrow that leads to life, and there are few who find it"* (Matthew 7:14) This less traveled, more difficult "road" is the living out of a spiritual life rather than a mere survival in our short passage through time. In exploring the inner meaning of spiritual teachings, it is necessary to go beyond the standard dogmas that are passed on through catechism, Sunday-school classes and theological seminaries. From the very beginning, there was an inner understanding of the teachings that had to be uncovered. Jesus said to his disciples: *"To you has been given the secret of the kingdom of God, but for those outside everything is in parables.*" (Mark 4:11) Contemporary theologians are very uncomfortable with this and they try to dismiss it along with other sayings such as "the Kingdom of God is within you" which is consistently translated "among you" because they cannot accept the implications of that little Greek preposition *en.*

But these are issues for scholastic minds lost in abstraction and afraid to enter the darkness of their own inner worlds. For people of the so-called *baby boom generation,* the awareness of other states of consciousness was never a serious problem. I entered upon my search for spiritual awakening in the mid-1970's, at a time when metaphysical literature and the discovery of eastern teachings were prime roadmaps for those who sought contact with greater meaning.

Out of what seemed like sheer coincidence, a book was lent to me by a friend at a time of particular need. It was a historical study of an ancient brotherhood of initiates who were brought into enlightenment in an age of great darkness. This was no plot for a second rate movie, but the lived experience of seekers from another era. I was especially struck by the fact that they were seeking for the same thing as I was: *a transformation of self into a consciousness of the deep mysteries of the human spirit and its cosmic origin.* This new life is the same in all centuries, in all cultures, in all religions: it is the Higher Self, which appears after the death of the little, invented, fragmented self. It is oneness, wholeness.

I soon began reading book after book: Eastern philosophy, esoteric teachings, and scientific studies on human consciousness, the spiritual mystics and lovers of God. The more I searched, the more I became certain that something was guiding me. The right book would fall into my hands at the right time. These books were food for my soul, creating a new life within, leading me onward toward a goal I knew nothing about, though I was beginning to realize in some mysterious way that there was something very great to be found.

One thing is certain: any search for transforming Truth, the kind that opens the inner sight to a radically new sense of reality, cannot be undertaken on the surface of our secular, materialistic society. That plane is made up exclusively of the search for food, mates, and success. It is the world of the absurd and the tragic, where people seem to be born in order to pay the rent, produce more consumers and workers for the anthill, and then die when their value as laborers is over. In such a life, there is no mystery, no wonder, no higher purpose, and no hope.

Those who intuitively recognize that this cannot possibly be the sum total of the purpose for existence must find their way into deeper undercurrents of civilization where another kind of knowledge is available to humanity, beyond the "eat or be eaten" syndrome. In other words, they must come upon "the road less traveled." Unfortunately, these subterranean levels include all sorts of quicksand and obstacles, and one must be prepared to struggle with dangerous traps in order to reach higher planes of understanding.

This blind hunger for experience of a wiser, vaster plane of reality comes from a deep inner yearning. It is particularly prevalent now that the worldview of the dominant cultures excludes this reality. Quite often, this need for experience of the transcendent is distorted into a return to the ancient world of omens and amulets, which seems more interesting than the world of shopping malls and fast food restaurants.

Then I met an old blind woman sitting behind a curtain in a darkened church who held my watch in her hand, concentrated on the energies it had absorbed from constant contact with my wrist, and told me that I would be taking a trip to Asia. Here I was, penniless, unemployed, without even the means to get to the nearest drugstore, and being told by a stranger that such a voyage would take place within a few months. The woman's simplicity, kindness, and down-home honesty kept me from classifying her as one more fraud along the way.

Then two months later, from completely out of the blue, I found myself sitting in an airplane on a thirty-two hour flight to Bangkok! Facts are hard to argue with. In this land of wandering monks, ever-present incense at roadside shrines, and underground temples dating back hundreds of years, it became all the more clear that returning to the rat-race of a greed-driven society was not the way to spend one's journey through this world.

The very rhythm of life was conducive to quiet

reflection. The exotic surroundings and ancient monuments confirmed that what I sought could be found. Human transformation was not simply a hot selling topic in *New Age* bookstores. It had been going on for centuries throughout the world, especially in these settings caressed by the gentle winds of the South China Sea.

During this brief interlude from the noise and madness of Western civilization, among elephants and monkeys, painted gods and peaceful shrines, I decided to devote my life to the search that had begun haphazardly in the haze of inner longing and alienation. The geography of the East materialized for me a new awareness of how different life could be from the hustle and bustle of the big cities I had frequented back home. I no longer had to rely on my imagination to invent some mythic world where higher consciousness was possible. Planet Earth is the stage where this evolution is meant to occur.

Back in the United States, I knew something was around the corner, something that would change the course of my life. I was now ready to sacrifice everything, even my childhood dreams, in order to walk that less traveled road and discover the wisdom which alone could show me the purpose of life and the way to contribute positively to the universe.

I was to discover the great irony that the very thing I ran away from—the Christian teachings—contained more mystery and wonder than anything I had experienced in my exotic wanderings.

The ancient Scriptures that are the foundation of Christianity invite us to seek after the mystery and power that we name God, but whose Name is too sacred to speak. They tell us that this unknown and yet very present Creative Force of the universe responds to us individually. But they add that a personal contact must be established to enable our participation in this new consciousness, that is, in order to walk the less traveled path into the "undiscovered country" of spirit.

The experience of encounter yields with the Divine generates a transformation, an awakening which opens onto another dimension of reality known in the symbolism of religious language as *life eternal*. *"And this is eternal life, that they <u>know</u> the only true God..." (John 17:3).*

This highest state of consciousness which the Apostle Paul described as "the peace that passes all understanding" (I like the translation – *"that no one understands"*) has been given many names.

At the turn of the century, Rudolf Otto named it *"the Mysterium Tremendum"* and R.M. Bucke called it *"cosmic consciousness."* Zen Buddhism names it *Satori*, in Yoga it is *Samadhi*, and in Taoism they know it as *"the absolute Tao."* In our day, Thomas Merton used the phrase *"transcendental unconscious"* while Abraham Maslow describes it as *"peak experience"*; the Sufis speak of *Fana* and G.I. Gurdjieff labeled it *"objective consciousness"* while the Quakers experience it as *"the Inner Light."* Karlfried Graf Dürckheim calls it the *"breakthrough of Being."*

What is meant by these mysterious expressions of the experience of enlightenment, illumination, liberation, mystical oneness? At its most basic level, we are dealing with a state of awareness that is radically different from our ordinary understanding. The word *mysticism*, so abused and rejected in mainstream religious circles, simply suggests an expansion of consciousness beyond the ordinary boundaries of our egos to a state where union with a greater reality is achievable. Evelyn Underhill defines mysticism as "the hunger for reality, the unwillingness to be satisfied with the purely animal or the purely social level of consciousness." This is the first and essential stage in the development of a mystical consciousness.

The less traveled road, or the mystic way as others might call it, is therefore a process of sublimation carrying the relationship of the self with the universe to higher levels than our ordinary states of awareness. But this is no selfish journey. For as the mystic grows nearer the source of true life and participates in the creative energies of the Divine, he or she is capable of greater unselfish activity to the point of unconditional Love.

We learn from the writings of the mystics that such a consciousness has the power to lift those who possess it to a plane of reality that no struggle, no cruelty, no catastrophe can disturb. This "inner sanctuary" is the point where God and the soul touch. In the fourteenth century, John Tauler referred to this place as "the ground of the soul." Catherine of Siena spoke of the "interior home of the heart," Teresa of Avila knew it as the "inner castle," and John of the Cross described it as the "house at rest in darkness and concealment."

These metaphors suggest a secret dwelling in the center of our being that remains permanently united with God's creative act. The self in its deepest nature is more than itself. To move into oneself means ultimately to move beyond oneself. But this does not wrap us in a selfish isolation from the pain and responsibility of life. Rather, it renews and empowers us to reach out to others in truly meaningful ways. Evelyn Underhill tells us that such inner transformation helps the mystics to enter, more completely than ever before, into the life of the group to which they belong:

> It *will teach them to see the world in a truer proportion, discerning eternal beauty beyond and beneath apparent ruthlessness. It will educate them in a charity free from all taint of sentimentalism; it will confer on them an unconquerable hope.*

Out of her vast study and personal experience, Underhill offers us one of the finest definitions of *mysticism*: "Mysticism is the way of union with Reality. The mystic is a person who has attained that union in greater or lesser degree; or who aims at and believes in such attainment."

Throughout Western history, most religious or spiritual teachings have emphasized the goal of human life and underplayed or neglected *the means by which this goal may be reached.* Jacob Needleman, a major contributor to the modern spiritual journey, asks the following question in his study of spirituality: what is the bridge that can lead a person from the state of submersion in egoistic emotions to that incomparable range of life known under the simple term "love of God"?

This is the journey of the one who chooses "the road less traveled" and there are many who have witnessed to the fact that this harder road, this narrow way, is an inner journey leading to the infinite depths of our True Self, crossing the threshold into becoming a conscious Child of God, a Child of the Universe.

Made in the USA
San Bernardino, CA
06 October 2016